REASON AND CULTURE

NEW PERSPECTIVES ON THE PAST

General Editor
R. I. Moore

Advisory Editors
Gerald Aylmer, Tanya Luhrmann, David Turley, Patrick Wormald

This series is designed to examine the broad issues and questions which are constantly touched upon in historical study, but are rarely examined directly. From a basis of sound and specific historical scholarship the authors explore their chosen themes, ranging widely across cultures and long periods of time, and often using the concepts and interpretations of other disciplines.

PUBLISHED

David Arnold   Famine
James Casey   The History of the Family
Patricia Crone   Pre-Industrial Societies
Ernest Gellner   Nations and Nationalism
Ernest Gellner   Reason and Culture
David Grigg   The Transformation of Agriculture in the West
Richard Hodges   Primitive and Peasant Markets
Eugene Kamenka   Bureaucracy
Edward Peters   Torture
Jonathan Powis   Aristocracy

IN PREPARATION

David Arnold   Culture and Environment
Richard Bonney   Absolutism
Bernard Crick   Representative Institutions
James Fentress and Chris Wickham   Social Memory
David Gress   The Modern State
Bernard Hamilton   Shrines
John MacKenzie   Hunting
Ian Simmonds   Wilderness
David Turley   Slavery

REASON AND CULTURE

THE HISTORIC ROLE OF RATIONALITY AND RATIONALISM

Ernest Gellner

BLACKWELL
Oxford UK & Cambridge USA

First published 1992

Blackwell Publishers
108 Cowley Road
Oxford OX4 1JF
UK

Three Cambridge Center
Cambridge, Massachusetts 02142
USA

A CIP catalogue record for this book is available from the British Library.

Library of Congress Cataloging-in-Publication Data

Gellner, Ernest.
Reason and culture: the historic
role of rationality and rationalism / Ernest Gellner.
p.   cm. — (New perspectives on the past)
Includes bibliographical references and index.
ISBN 0–631–13479–4 — ISBN 0–631–13711–4 (pbk.)
1. Sociology – Philosophy.   2. Reason.   3. Rationalism.   I. Title.
II. Series: New perspectives on the past (Basil Blackwell Publishers)
HM24.G425   1922
301'.01 – dc20   91–27067
                                                    CIP

ISBN 0–631–13479–4
0–631–13711–4 (pbk)

Typeset in 11 on 13 pt Plantin
by Graphicraft Typesetters Ltd., Hong Kong
Printed in Great Britain by Biddles Ltd., Guildford Surrey

This book is printed on acid-free paper.

For Mary McGinley and Gaye Woolven

Contents

Editor's Preface

Ignorance has many forms, and all of them are dangerous. In the nineteenth and twentieth centuries our chief effort has been to free ourselves from tradition and superstition in large questions, and from the error in small ones upon which they rest, by redefining the fields of knowledge and evolving in each the distinctive method appropriate for its cultivation. The achievement has been incalculable, but not without cost. As each new subject has developed a specialist vocabulary to permit rapid and precise reference to its own common and rapidly growing stock of ideas and discoveries, and come to require a greater depth of expertise from its specialists, scholars have been cut off by their own erudition not only from mankind at large, but from the findings of workers in other fields, and even in other parts of their own. Isolation diminishes not only the usefulness but the soundness of their labours when energies are exclusively devoted to eliminating the small blemishes so embarrassingly obvious to the fellow-professional on the next patch, instead of avoiding others that may loom much larger from, as it were, a more distant vantage point. Marc Bloch observed a contradiction in the attitudes of many historians: 'when it is a question of ascertaining whether or not some human act has really taken place, they cannot be too painstaking. If they proceed to the reasons for that act, they are content with the merest appearance, ordinarily founded upon one of those maxims of common-place psychology which are neither more nor less true that their opposites.' When the historian peeps across the fence he sees his neighbours, in literature, perhaps, or sociology, just as complacent in relying on historical platitudes which are naive, simplistic or obsolete.

New Perspectives on the Past represents not a reaction against specialization, which would be a romantic absurdity, but an attempt to come to terms with it. The authors, of course, are specialists, and their thought and conclusions rest on the foundation of distinguished professional research in different periods and fields. Here they will free themselves, as far as it is possible, from the constraints of subject, region and period within which they ordinarily and necessarily work, to discuss problems simply as problems, and not as 'history' or 'politics' or 'economics'. They will write for specialists, because we are all specialists now, and for laymen, because we are all laymen.

Cogito ergo sum: if the modern world has a beginning it is there. The 'Age of Reason' dethroned authority in religion and politics, and laid the foundations of a society based on the apparently limitless increase of wealth through the systematic comprehension and exploitation of nature. In doing so it brought about a decisive rupture with the traditional world – including not only its own past but those parts of the modern world which did not share in the benefits of European Progress – giving us both the medicines which have enabled us to sustain ourselves and the ills which we have failed to cure.

Every student knows Descartes's words, but it is not so easy to understand why or how they have changed the world. That is not a question only for historians or philosophers, for the nature and limits of rational enquiry lie at the heart of mathematics and physics, of sociology and psychology, of all the natural and social sciences. It is not a question only for scholars and intellectuals, for whether reason can claim a unique ascendancy, in preference over other forms of guidance, lies at the heart of human and social identity, and of moral and political action. If Ernest Gellner had contented himself with describing how the dilemma which Descartes posed between the sovereignty of reason and the claims of culture – that is, of the entire human inheritance beyond the merely genetic – shaped the next three centuries of Western thought, he would have written a book of great importance. He has gone beyond that to propose a bold and powerful resolution of the last and most agonizing dilemma with which reason has seemed to confront its modern disciples: whether reason itself is merely another kind of superstition. In consequence this is a book which for many of its readers will provide not only a New Perspective on the Past, but new hope for the future.

R. I. Moore

Acknowledgements

This volume could not have been written without the extremely generous support of the staff of the Social Anthropology Department office at Cambridge – Mrs Mary McGinley, Mrs Margaret Story, Mrs Anne Farmer and Mr Humphrey Hinton. Miss Sarah Green also provided most valuable help. Their help included typing, checking of references, bibliography, mastery of recalcitrant modern equipment, and general moral support enabling one to write whilst under stress from other obligations. I am also grateful for editorial help and assistance to John Davey, Robert Moore, Sue Martin and Ginny Stroud-Lewis.

On the financial side, I am much indebted to the Economic and Social Research Council and its then Chairman, Sir Douglas Hague, for a grant intended to facilitate theoretical research, and, for a similar grant, to the Nuffield Foundation and its Assistant Director, Miss Patricia Thomas. This study is in effect part of a wider and on-going effort to contribute to the theory of contemporary social change, an endeavour which would have been that much harder without the support received. Needless to say, the responsibility for the views expressed is mine alone.

E.G.
Cambridge, November 1991

Our reason must be considered as a kind of cause, of which truth is the natural effect...

David Hume

...bei vielen...ein gewisser Grad von Misologie, d.i. Hass der Vernunft entspringt, weil sie...finden, dass sie sich in der Tat mehr Muehseligkeit gezogen als Glueckseligkeit gewonnen haben, und darueber endlich den gemeinern Schlag der Menschen...der seiner Vernunft nicht viel Einfluss...verstattet, eher beneiden, all geringschaetzen.

Many develop a certain measure of misology, i.e. hatred of reason, because they find that they had won weariness for themselves rather than bliss, and so in the end they tend to envy, rather than despise, the commoner run of men, who grant but little influence to their reason...

Immanuel Kant

C'est la raison humaine qui a renversé toutes les illusions; mais elle en porte elle-même le deuil, afin qu'on la console.

It is human reason which has destroyed all illusions; but reason herself wears mourning for it, so as to induce us to console her.

Alfred de Musset

1
Reason and Culture

The curse of custom and example

> We ought never to allow ourselves to be persuaded of the truth of
> anything unless on the evidence of our reason.[1]

This affirmation of the sovereignty of Reason is as good a brief
summary of rationalism as we can desire. René Descartes was
probably the greatest rationalist ever. Moreover, he was also a
tormented one. Submission to Reason does not bring immediate
and total inner peace, if indeed it brings peace at all. Descartes's
thought is, fortunately for us, expressed in poignant autobio-
graphical form. The simultaneously disturbing and comforting
role which Reason played in his life is made exceeding plain:

> ...many things which, however extravagant and ridiculous to our
> apprehension, are yet by common consent received and approved
> by other great nations...[2]

A little later he makes the same point even more strongly:

---

[1] René Descartes, *Discourse on Method*, part IV (first published 1637). For
modern editions of this and other works cited, see the Select Bibliography.
[2] ibid., part I.

> ...no opinion, however absurd and incredible, can be imagined, which has not been maintained by some one of the philosophers... in the course of my travels I remarked that all those whose opinions are decidedly repugnant to ours are not on that account barbarians and savages, but on the contrary...many of these nations make an equally good, if not better, use of their reason than we do. ...the ground of our opinion is far more *custom and example* than any certain knowledge.[1]

Extravagant and ridiculous beliefs are held by other nations. Who are we to think we are exempt from confident delusion? The argument from illusion is formulated by Descartes, as it properly should be, in terms of entire cultures, rather than of individual error. What is disturbing is not that *I* am liable to err, but that the shared assumptions of an entire society, built into its way of life and sustained by it, should be deeply misguided. Entire societies are deeply committed, with fervour and often with arrogance and with infuriating complacency, to blatant absurdities. This being so, how can we trust our own strong collective conviction? We know *them* to be fools. Are we ourselves exempt from folly? Why should we hold ourselves to be exempt from such fallibility?

In the light of this, Descartes decides to become sceptical concerning anything 'of the truth of which I had been persuaded merely by *example and custom*'.[2] Liberation from error requires liberation from culture, from 'example and custom' as he calls it. It is this accumulation of complacent, confident conviction, and its acceptance, which leads men into error. There must be another and a better way.

Liberation is to be achieved by purification through *doubt*: that which is based only on custom and example is dubitable but, he eventually concludes, that which is rational is not. Culture and Reason are antithetical. Culture is questionable, Reason is not. Doubt and Reason must jointly purge our minds of that which is merely cultural, accidental and untrustworthy.

---

[1] ibid., part II; my italics.
[2] ibid., part I; my italics.

Descartes disclaims any ambition to be a general or political reformer. He assures us that his aspiration is more modest, or so it would seem at first sight:

> I have never contemplated anything higher than the reformation of my own opinions, and basing them on foundations *wholly my own*.[1]

So Descartes's rationalism is also profoundly individualist: one can, he claims, construct a world on foundations that are not only rational but *wholly one's own*. It is the use of foundations laid by others which leads to error. The rational is the private, and perhaps the private is also to be the rational...

So individualism and rationalism are closely linked: that which is collective and customary is non-rational, and the overcoming of unreason and of collective custom are one and the same process. Descartes wishes, cognitively speaking, to be a self-made man. He is the Samuel Smiles of cognitive enterprise. Error is to be found in culture; and culture is a kind of systematic, communally induced error. It is of the essence of error that it is communally induced and historically accumulated. It is through community and history that we sink into error, and it is through solitary design and plan that we escape it. Truth is acquired in a planned orderly manner by an individual, not slowly gathered up by a herd. Complete individual intellectual autarchy is, it would seem, feasible. It had better be, for it is our salvation.

In any case, Descartes proposes to attempt to achieve it. In fact, he thinks he has made quite a good job of it, good enough to warrant presenting it to the public. But he does not wish to encourage all and sundry to follow his example. This is not really something suitable for everyone:

> ...my own satisfaction with my work has led me to present here a draft of it, I do not by any means therefore commend to everyone else to make a similar attempt.[2]

---

[1] ibid., part II; my italics.
[2] ibid., part II.

Apart from being individualist, Descartes's liberation-seeking, culture-defying rationalism is both classicist and bourgeois. These traits are interrelated. His classicism consists of a marked preference for buildings, legal systems, opinions and so forth that are deliberately designed by a single author. It is good for a thing to be born of a clear and deliberate plan. Such creations are to be preferred to those which merely grow, by gradual and unplanned accretion. Not for him the romantic affection for an ancient, slowly matured set of practices, institutions, structures, endowed with a mellow wisdom that is half as old as time.

> ...ancient cities...are usually but ill laid out compared with the regularly constructed towns which a professional architect has freely planned on an open plain. ...nations...advancing to civilisation by slow degrees...would by this process come to be possessed of less perfect institutions than those which...have followed the appointments of some wise legislator.[1]

Consistently with such a view, he deems it a pity that the ordinary human process of maturation actually obliges us to grow, and thus share in that corruption which is the fruit of growth. It would have been better by far if reason alone, rather than organic growth, had formed us:

> ...it is almost impossible that our judgements can be so correct or solid as they would have been, had our reason been mature from the moment of our birth...[2]

Infancy, youth and maturation are a kind of original corrupting sin. In effect, they are *the* sin of thought. They expose us to custom and example, at a time when we are ill-equipped to resist them, for in our immaturity we know no better and they permeate us. It would be better by far if our ideas were the results of the implementation of a clear and conscious design, rather than, as

[1] ibid., part II.
[2] ibid., part II.

is the case, the culmination of a long and unplanned process of maturation.

It would be better still if we were to design and plan *ourselves*! Descartes is about to try to do precisely that. He will redesign himself, or at least the part of himself he cares for most – his ideas concerning the world. In a secular sense, he intends to be twice-born. The second time round he will be his own author, and fully responsible for what he thinks and knows. The new, regenerate, twice-born rationalist self, however, will be brought forth not by faith but by doubt.

If only we could be born complete! To be the product of slow unselfconscious growth is to be impure. Descartes is totally innocent of that romanticism which sees deep wisdom in slow and unconscious growth, and great beauty in the unplanned fruits of gradual adaptation. He is more than free of it, he disavows it with emphasis. History is pollution.

He is also profoundly bourgeois. The rules which he sets out for the comportment, both of his mind and of his person, in the course of execution of any design, and in particular of his favoured design of cognitive self-creation, convey the very essence of the middle-class spirit. It is of course quite specially important to observe these rules in the radical reconstruction of self. Then above all, let us have no haste, no untidy confusion, no impulsiveness. All precipitancy and prejudice are to be avoided; all issues are to be divided into as many parts as possible; and one is to proceed with maximum orderliness from the simple to the complex, and practise a conceptual accountancy so complete and so general that one 'might be assured that nothing had been omitted'.[1] It is indeed in such a spirit that the bourgeois entrepreneur deploys his resources and keeps his accounts and records in financial and legal order – slow, careful, judicious, deliberate, omitting naught, accounting for all. Do but one thing at a time. Subject the performance to an accurate and searching accountancy, which judges it by clear, intelligible criteria. Descartes is

---

[1] ibid., part II.

the outstanding practitioner and preacher of a cognitive Possess-
ive Individualism.

The individualism, the classicism and the bourgeois spirit are
all closely linked. The classicism, insisting on conscious design
and clear criteria, admirably complements the bourgeois sense
of order. Rigorous accountancy is hardly possible without clear
criteria and measures. The individualism is an expression of a
need for self-sufficiency, a yearning for freedom from any kind
of indebtedness: he will not mortgage his convictions to some
communal bank of custom, whose management is outside his
control, and which consequently is not really to be trusted, for
it cannot be personally, individually checked for soundness.
(Debtors are liable to be under pressure and they make suspect
witnesses; cognitive debtors cannot be credited with integrity
of judgement.) Collectivism inclines those under its sway to
opportunistic compromise, its commitment to multiple and
imprecise criteria precludes accurate cost-benefit accountancy.
Even when the 'constitution of the true religion' is commended
by Descartes, it is done in a way which makes plain that its
superiority lies at least as much in the orderly centralization of
the divine practice and pronouncement as in any special status
of the Designer. This, he clearly feels, was a neat and tidy Revelation, not one of your customary hotch-potch communal
religions. It is the concentration of Revelation in a single point,
and the unification of the sacred hierarchy at its single authoritative apex, which he finds appealing in the religion into which he
was born, rather than its traditionalism, or its historic fusion with
the life of a community. The latter kind of attraction, due to
become so very fashionable later on, did not move him at all.

There is more than a touch of anguish in Descartes's wrestling
with his problems. That too, perhaps, is well in the tradition of
the early bourgeoisie, if Max Weber is to be believed. It was inner
struggle, anxiety and doubt which in Weber's view made the early
capitalists so orderly, systematic, and persistent, and which made
them accumulate wealth as fastidiously and doggedly as Descartes
strove to accumulate truths. What tormented Descartes, admit-

tedly, was not that he might be damned, but that he might be mistaken. His anguish was intellectual not spiritual. But Descartes hardly distinguished between the two. For a true intellectual, one devoted to ideas and truth above all things, error is the very essence of damnation. Other kinds of deprivation do not matter much. Descartes's life was so very much the life of the mind that for him error was not the cause of damnation, but damnation itself.

Descartes's wrestling with God, which takes up a significant part of his writings, has a rather special quality. Like Job, René Descartes is smitten by the problem of evil. But for him the problem takes on a very special form. He does not appear to be so very much disturbed by all the terrible injustice which can and does occur in God's world. He took part in one of the most vicious and brutal wars in the history of Europe, but the experience does not seem to have scarred him. It is one injustice in particular, or indeed its sheer possibility, which troubles him above all else: the injustice of suffering *error*. How could God endow us with mental powers, and yet allow us to err? How could one live in the shadow of such cruelty? It was this possibility which Descartes found intolerable, and he was clearly determined to clear the deity of so terrible a suspicion. *The one activity in the world which really does concern Descartes is thought and the pursuit of truth*. Had he composed the Lord's Prayer, it would no doubt have contained the invocation 'and lead us not into error'!

It is evil in this sphere, the occurrence of *undeserved* error, that constitutes something for which Descartes, in his heart, could never have forgiven God. Injury to human fortune and person is something which, it would seem, we ought to bear with stoic fortitude. But injury to the human mind, in the form of error, is something Descartes cannot endure with equanimity. The idea that error might be our lot though we had not deserved it is not to be borne. Undeserved misery is tolerable, undeserved error is not.

Happily he convinces himself that he need not endure it. God is quite innocent of the intellectual errors committed by His creatures. He has made it perfectly possible for them to avoid error: if they fall into it none the less, it is their own fault, and not His.

If God is not guilty of bringing error into the world, who then is the culprit?

> ...the chief cause of our errors is to be found in the prejudices of our childhood.[1]

It is the involvement of the immature mind in the world which engenders a mass of false beliefs:

> ...our mind has been imbued from infancy with a thousand other prejudices of the same sort...[2]

Though his official account of error is somewhat individualistic, describing it as something which occurs in the growth of his single mind, Descartes also knows full well that the pervasive pattern of error varies from society to society. It is produced by what he described as *custom and example*. Thou shalt not follow a multitude to commit error. But most of us do precisely that. The enemy is evidently our socialization, our inclusion in a culture. Salvation on the other hand lies in individual re-examination of our ideas:

> ...we must take care scrupulously to withhold our assent from the opinions we have formerly admitted...[3]

The battle-lines are now clear: it is individual reason versus collective culture. Truth can be secured only by stepping outside prejudice and accumulated custom, and refashioning one's world. It can only be achieved by means of proudly independent, solitary Reason. We pursue it rationally, and we do it alone.

But what methods does reason deploy in this formidable

---

[1] René Descartes, *The Principles of Philosophy*, LXXI (first published 1644).
[2] ibid.
[3] ibid., LXXV.

struggle? In brief, it can rely on inner compulsion. To be precise, and this nuance is extremely important, it can rely on inner compulsion *of a certain restricted kind*. Not any compulsion, but only a rather special kind of compulsion, supplies the mind with its crucial touchstone of truth and rationality.

Descartes admits that we can easily conceive that neither God nor the sky nor bodies nor our own body exist. All these might well be part and parcel of our infantile and collective, customary prejudices. The existence of these entities fails the stringent test of indubitability, which he had himself proposed as the means of our decontamination from cultural superstition.

It is the affirmation of the existence of a thinking being which alone allows Descartes, whilst formulating the most famous argument of modern times, to escape the constriction of merely custom-born conviction. That argument asserts – *I think, therefore I am*. That one affirmation, that truth, *does* pass the test. It does so unscathed:

> ...there is a *repugnance* in conceiving that what thinks does not exist at the very time it thinks.[1]

Thus it is an irresistible inner repugnance towards the rejection of a certain idea, or, more positively, an inner compulsion to accept it, which liberates Descartes from the bitterly resented and fatal, error-infected dependency on mere custom and example, on society and culture. Irresistible inner compulsion alone provides the Archimedean fixed point that enables us to escape enslavement to contingent and socially variable custom, which enables us to liberate ourselves from error by providing us with our untainted, decontaminated starting point. So there is at least one idea which has the power to impose itself on us *come what may*, irrespective of whatever accidental pressures may have been imposed upon us by historic and cultural contingency. Cultural brainwashing, however thorough, cannot affect that luminous island of self-sustaining certainty. An escape from contingent custom and example is feasible after all.

---

[1] ibid., VII; my italics.

But note that it is only the better kind of compulsion, and not any old compulsion, which can claim the exalted role of liberator of the human mind from error. Only the pure kind of compulsion can liberate us. It is the compulsion which attaches to clear and distinct ideas, and it alone, which has this elevated and liberating quality. Not compulsion as such, but lucid and distinct compulsion, is legitimate, trustworthy and liberating.

The most important point about Descartes's account of the human condition is this: in order to avail oneself of reason, and to escape from culture, one must transcend all the error which culture instils, and one must heed the inner compulsions of a special kind. One must heed them, and one must heed no others. The appropriate slogan for Descartes's version of liberation philosophy is *selective compulsion*. It is the better kind of inner compulsion which alone can deliver us from evil. It is a compulsion which arises only after we have observed his bourgeois rules for the comportment of our understanding – slow deliberation, clarity, separation of issues, thoroughness, accountability, auditing.

The inner appeal of the famous principle 'I think, therefore I am' is, for Descartes, the supreme and crucial example of such compulsion-by-lucid-ideas. He claimed that no man could refuse it his assent. It was the very model of legitimate, valid inner compulsion. It is quite particularly compelling; and thereby it sets a standard and a precedent and a starting point, all at once. Such truths, and such truths alone, are fit to guide us.

This crucial example also illustrates just why it is itself compelling and cogent: because each of its constituents is itself clear and distinct. This allows Descartes to generalize the connection between clarity and cogency, or so he believes. It enables him to conclude that *all* such clear and distinct ideas are similarly sound and reliable, even if this one is more so, somehow self-generating and self-validating. It sets a precedent, it shows that cognitive trustworthiness is available.

At the same time, the existence of the thinking self remains rather special: it alone was compulsive from the start, even *before* that generalization based on its recognition had been formulated and accepted. It made the attainment of that generalization possible; and yet it was itself a kind of illuminating, shining example, and extended its own legitimacy to all those ideas capable of following or emulating its precedent. It was, in a somewhat new sense, the immaculate conception, untainted by mundane corruption.

From the existence of the thinking self, Descartes infers (by a most dubious procedure which satisfies him, but which does not concern us) the existence of a God; and, proceeding further from the premiss of the goodness of a God who could not be a deceiver, he concludes in turn that clear and distinct ideas in general cannot mislead us. Thus the deity, having had Its own existence established by one set of such clear and distinct ideas, obligingly returns the compliment, and confers authenticated trustworthiness on them all.

At the same time, this solves the problem of evil, in the form in which it most troubles Descartes: how is error possible in a world ruled by a benign God? Answer: God has endowed us with clear and distinct ideas. Had we followed them, we should be error-free. It is not *His* fault that we follow culture, custom and example, and fall into error.

Descartes's cognitive world is a kind of dual monarchy, within which it is hard to say whether it is lucid reason or the deity that is the ultimate sovereign. Each of them confirms the authority of the other, and they rule jointly. Neither could rule alone. The deity needs clear and distinct ideas so as to have Its own reality established. A set of clear and distinct ideas establishes the existence of God. Clear and distinct ideas in general, however, need the deity, so that the initially exiguous bridgehead of reason be extended. Only thus is it possible to underwrite *all* clear and distinct ideas.

Only one clear and distinct idea, the existence of the thinking (conscious) self, is established autonomously, without any extraneous aid whatever, not even that of the deity. The existence of the self and of its idea of God then establish the *existence* of the deity, which in turn then underwrites the reliability of all *other* clear ideas. Now the world is at last accessible to reliable knowledge; and error can be avoided by those who follow the true path of reason.

The details of Descartes's solution do not really concern us. They are of historic interest only. What is of great and permanent relevance is his general characterization of the human condition. Man is helplessly at the mercy of false, custom-born ideas, instilled in him by his social environment in the course of his education. He can only extricate himself from them with the greatest difficulty. But extricate himself he must! How? By attending to his inner compulsions. But not to all of them: he must heed only those which display and observe the highest standards of lucidity, of logical cogency.

Note that the deity which underwrites the reliability of these compulsions, is Itself an exceedingly bourgeois deity. It is carefully selective in what it underwrites: it provides no charter at all for murky, turbulent, obscure inner compulsions. It is not at all the kind of deity which reveals itself through trance, or some mystic or orgiastic dissolution of conceptual order. It does not favour emotional excess amongst its devotees, and certainly does not propose to reveal Itself unto them in the course of any such undecorous indulgence. Such forms of communication it leaves to other and presumably spurious faiths and sects.

It could in fact hardly be further removed from a spiritual Being who favoured such dissolute channels of communication with mankind. It certainly does not commend infantile simplicity or emotional abandon as paths of access to Itself. This deity has as great an aversion as does Descartes himself to what later came to be called romanticism. It would have no truck with violent emotion or deliberate excess as paths to illumination. It would not condone the use of hysteria, especially if induced by artificial means. It grants Its imprimatur to inner compulsions only in as far as these are orderly, clear, distinct, systematic – in brief, *rationally* compelling. This is a God of order, sobriety and reason.

The very same virtues which Descartes imposed on himself in the course of his inquiry are evidently also those which the deity favours in the inner life of Its creatures. So long as those rules are obeyed in deciding which inner impulsions to obey and which to disregard, no error will occur. Hence the deity is not accountable for error, and cognitive grace is available to all. It is available to all men by their own efforts: Descartes would seem to be Pelagian.

So Descartes's rather special version of the problem of evil, the problem of *error*, is solved. This is Descartes's theodicy: it is not the deity, but only our disregard for the rules It had implicitly instilled in us for the conduct of our understanding, which is to blame for error. Error is the only kind of evil that genuinely troubles Descartes. Inner Compulsions of a Clear and Distinct Kind can overcome it: they, and they alone, provide the safe handrail to cognitive salvation.

Reason against Culture

Descartes initiated a programme for escaping unreliable, accidentally acquired conviction. In effect, he proposed a programme for man's liberation from culture. This was to be achieved by means of a proper understanding of what was, and what was not, legitimately available to our minds. This strategy was perpetuated by others and completed in the eighteenth century by David Hume and Immanuel Kant. But the spirit of the inquiry and its implicit terms of reference remained much as Descartes had formulated them: the individualist, classicist, bourgeois spirit, un-romantic, anti-communal and un-historical, continued to pervade the exercise and provide it with its tacit assumptions. A good deal changed, however, in the details of its implementation.

A series of British empiricists, of whom Hume was the culmination, replaced *concepts* by *perceptions* as the basic building-blocks of the edifice of knowledge. Individual consciousness was still to be the foundation of everything, but its content was seen as fleeting sense impressions, and not some putative ego-substance, as Descartes had claimed.

This did not, however, affect the basic strategy, the understanding of the human condition. Descartes trusted 'ideas' because they were ours, given, inwardly manifest; the empiricist trusted perceptions or sensations for the very same reason. Either way, a private and inescapable data base was to be the foundation of a new edifice. The central position of the empiricists continued to imply a culture-defying individualism, a Robinson Crusoe posture, an ability and willingness to make one's own world. In politics, Hume combined this with a certain respect for ongoing traditions; but this did not modify his central intuition – namely, that the world was constructed from private data of consciousness, and hence that, by examining what those data really contained, we could determine what was and was not to be found in the world.

So sensualism replaces conceptualism within this overall programme. We know through our senses: the mind itself only retains, or accumulates, but it does not engender any knowledge. Descartes could only view with contempt the scholastic dictum that there was nothing in the mind which had not previously been in the senses. In his estimation, the reverse was almost closer to the truth: the most valuable content of the mind had indeed never passed through the senses. In his return to sensualism, Hume by contrast went even further than the famous dictum: for him, concepts or ideas were nothing but the aftertaste of sensations. The pursuit of the luminously self-authenticating clarity and distinctiveness of Descartes's *ideas* is abandoned. There are no self-validating ideas. Ideas are justified, and can only be justified, by the perceptions which had fathered them. But the perceptions retain the function which ideas had possessed for Descartes. It amounts to much the same. They can perform that role in the same way in which ideas had performed it: they are inescapably, inevitably, compulsively present in *us* individually. They provide us with an individual basis by means of which we can censor cultural claims. Culture can be transcended by the cognitive Robinson Crusoe. And before they can perform the task assigned to them, they are subjected to the same purification as the one Descartes imposed on ideas: they are atomized, broken up into their elementary constituents. Item-by-item scrutiny is imposed in the cognitive audit.

Hume, like Descartes, is eager to distinguish what we can

genuinely claim to know from that which we cannot. Like
Descartes, he had in effect a single and simple touchstone. But it
was no longer quite the same one; it was no longer distinctness
and clarity of ideas, and the inner compulsiveness which allegedly they bring. For Hume, the touchstone is different; it is a
principle which he claims to have established by introspection.
The principle is that all ideas are in the end nothing but the
echoes of impressions. No cognition without impression: this he
claims to have established by observation. Knowledge has no
other sources. So the touchstone for the validity of an idea is the
genuine availability of its genitor-impression.

Hume also denies that there is any very radical difference,
other than vividness, between ideas and impressions. Ideas are
simply feeble echoes of impressions. For Hume, this constitutes
both one of his conclusions *and*, in the actual structure of his
thought, the principal premiss for securing all other conclusions.
Ideas/echoes are feeble, and impressions/ancestors are vivid; and
there is no legitimate offspring without a vivid progenitor. By
inspecting the roll-call of ancestors in our vivid sensory stream,
we can tell which echo/ideas may be granted a right of residence
in our mind. By this method, we determine the legitimate,
justified limits of our world, and prune it of spurious, illegitimate
accretions.

Hume employs this rule for the same end, and in much the
same way, as Descartes had used his principle of the validity of
clear and distinct ideas. The programme remains even if its
execution is modified. He uses it so as to sort out the sheep from
the goats, to separate that which we could justifiably believe from
that which we could not. The validating *lettre de noblesse* of an idea
is its documented descent from an ancestral impression.

In one important sense, Hume is of course not a rationalist at
all: he is conventionally classed as an empiricist, and as such, as a
thinker opposed to rationalism. None the less, the key terms of
reference of the Cartesian enterprise are retained. Hume remains
a rationalist in a crucial sense: we see in him an individualistic
attempt to set up rationally the limits and nature of the genuinely
knowable world.

There is indeed some change of stress: Descartes, though believing that all men are endowed with the Reason which will save them from error if only they would use it aright, none the less knows he is constructing a *new* world. He lived amongst men who had not yet followed his path of cognitive salvation, and who were unfamiliar with the barely emerging scientific world. To a much greater extent, by contrast, Hume believed that he was recording the manner in which some men at least had actually come to think: namely, those who lived in the new Galilean world, shared by the men of the Enlightenment. He was no longer setting up as a cognitive Crusoe: instead, he was codifying the cognitive rules of a world which already existed, a world shared by the community of the enlightened.

The difference is less one between Descartes and Hume than between their times. Men had changed during the hundred or so years that had passed. Descartes lived through, and indeed had fought in – if in a somewhat lukewarm manner – the last though the bloodiest of the Wars of Religion. Whilst sitting out a harsh winter in a cosy billet, squatting by his stove, his mind clearly turned to cognitive, rather than to military, strategy. Hume by contrast lived in the Augustan age, with its limited highly professional wars. He had actually taken part, in a secretarial capacity, in an amazingly humane and virtually bloodless campaign. A besieged French garrison had come out to surrender to a British force, whom they considered too formidable to resist. Their intention, however, was thwarted and they failed to surrender, because they found no one to whom they could surrender: the British force had in the meantime withdrawn, because they had concluded the French position to be so formidable as to be impregnable.[1] One can hardly think of a more humane – indeed truly enlightened – engagement.

But let us return to the activity for which these two men are more renowned than they are for their military pursuits, symptomatic though their respective wars were of their times – namely

---

[1] cf. E.C. Mossner, *The Life of David Hume*, 2nd edn (Clarendon Press, Oxford, 1980).

thinking. Descartes recorded how one man in his solitude *did* think, and how in his view others *should* think. Hume was recording how both he and many others already thought. Although he knew that other styles of thought also existed, and deplored them, his interest in these other styles was not central to his work.

There are various interesting differences between Descartes and Hume, but perhaps the most important is this: Descartes had attained, or thought he had attained, not without anguish, both a solid self and a safe world. Hume was never altogether sure that he had acquired either. Descartes supposed that his rationalist enterprise could be and was successful. Relying on nothing other than ideas held by him to be self-authenticating through their clarity and distinctness, he thought he could establish, first, the existence of a comfortably substantial self, and then, indirectly, through the intermediary of a cognitive-underwriter-God, an orderly, reliable, and cognizable world. Though self and world had some marked difficulty in communicating with each other (a difficulty that would haunt his philosophic posterity), none the less there was between them a deep harmony, sympathy, and complementarity. The world was reliably knowable by the self. There was no question of the self being brutally thrown into a world which it had never made, which it was ill-equipped either to know or to understand, and which was hostile to it.

Such an anguished vision was not yet on the scene, or at least had not attained *its* overt and sustained literary expression. The Cartesian self, its own solid substantial existence firmly established, entered the world well and fully equipped to know and understand that world. The world was there to receive it, and was cognitively available to it. The tools with which the self had been equipped from on high were of such excellent quality that, provided they were properly deployed, in accordance with the Master's instructions which had somehow accompanied them (though they were only properly read by Descartes), cognitive efforts could never encounter failure, humiliation, and distress. Success was guaranteed if the instructions were properly followed. If the mind used them improperly (which alas was what most men did), well it only had itself to blame. But if it behaved properly, it was safe. At the end of the day, it could confidently expect its reward. It could know the world securely, and there was also to be a secure and proper place for it in the world. Descartes had solved at least the cognitive version of the problem of evil to his own satisfaction.

Note well what Descartes had done: in truly rationalist spirit, he decided to declare independence of the accidental assemblage of beliefs, of all cultural accretion, and to set out independently on a re-exploration of the world. Culture, a shared set of ideas, held to be valid simply because they constituted the joint conceptual banks of custom of an ongoing community, is spurned. It is spurned *because* it is culture. Its social and customary origin is *the* fatal taint.

But at the putative end of his rationalist enterprise, Descartes thinks he has recovered precisely that very boon which cultures bestow on their members/participants: the warm gratification of possessing both a self and a world, which jointly dovetail and interlock, and which mutually support and underwrite each other. Each of them possesses a kind of authorized, guaranteed, vindicated status, and they reinforce each other. The world is there to be known and appreciated by the self, the self has its best aspirations supported and endorsed by the world. Happy members of well-integrated cultures normally have precisely such a feeling, though they may not formulate it to themselves in such words.

Descartes evidently believed that he could go it alone, and finally return to an individually erected intellectual edifice endowed precisely with those moral and conceptual comforts which are traditionally bestowed on men only by historic collectivities, by 'custom and example'. They were to be just as comfortable, yet this time their comforts would be self-made, reliable, and trustworthy, and not just inherited, taken over from highly suspect, untrustworthy cultural ancestors. By individualist, rationalist means, he hopefully expected to attain all the privileges of a well-endowed historic culture.

What if the availability of all this confidence and mutual support is but an illusion? What if it has been the age-old function of cultures to supply mankind with illusions? What if, without a culture, such a comfortable conceptual habitation simply was not to be had? What if we can have either confidence and moral support, *or* cognitive growth, but never the two at once? What if a society was to emerge which lived by cognitive growth, which consequently was committed to respecting Descartes's criteria, but which, in its vision of the world, could never see those criteria satisfied?

If all this is so, then Descartes is endeavouring to achieve the impossible. He is trying to make his own knowledge of the world independent of his culture, and indeed of *any* culture; and at the same time he tries to endow it with those very characteristics whose reality or illusionary presence – probably the latter – can only be engendered and sustained by a culture. These cognitive comforts are just the kind of thing which cultures, and cultures alone, can produce. By the end of the pursuit of the adventure of reason, we may well come to the conclusion, not merely that these two aspirations of Descartes's are incompatible with each other, but also that neither of them on its own can be satisfied. Perhaps there can be no culture-free cognition, any more than there can be a genuine vindication of any world. We cannot escape a contingent, history-bound culture; and we cannot vindicate it either. Descartes had thought that he *could* indeed vindicate a vision, *and* that it could be a vision not indebted to the contingencies of history, of custom and example.

What may be possible is that mankind should attain a form of cognition which, though still culture-bound, is bound to a wholly new *kind* of culture (and one unwittingly heralded and exemplified by Descartes); and that this form of cognition is far more potent than any earlier forms of knowledge; and that, as part of the price of such power, it is obliged to shed the illusion that it can vindicate itself, and moreover, it will *not* be comfortable, and cannot ever recover comfort. Feeling securely at home in the world is something that will not be granted to it.

The missing charter

The really important difference between Hume and Descartes is that Hume had come to perceive the acute difficulty of vindicating, underwriting, guaranteeing the world attained by rational exploration. Hume is famous as the thinker who highlighted the difficulties inherent in any attempt to justify our convictions.

Descartes's one and only really clear and distinct and self-vindicating idea, the existence of the thinking self, turns in the hands of the British empiricists into the indubitability of the immediate data of consciousness, of sensations. All these manifold activities which Descartes listed –

> ...a thinking thing...that doubts, understands, affirms, denies, wills, refuses,...imagines...perceives...[1]

– are now transformed into perceptions, into impressions and ideas. The self ceases to be a premiss; instead, it becomes merely the location, or perhaps the name, for our ultimate data base.

Hume explored the ways in which a habitable, usable, entrepreneur-worthy world might be constructed or attained from so exiguous a base as a mere assemblage of perceptions. His conclusion was that the transition from such a data base to the orderly habitable world was exceedingly precarious – and it could not in any circumstances be guaranteed. Those who made the transition did so – not so much at their own peril, for they had little choice in the matter – but simply because it was their *custom* to do so. So the custom, which Descartes had spurned so fiercely as a foundation of knowledge, turned out in the end to be quite indispensable for the construction of a world, after all. But by such custom, Hume still meant not something socially variable, culturally specific, but something pervading all human minds.

The manner in which we proceed from the ephemeral, transient, fragmentary and discontinous world of our immediate data, to a persistent, orderly, fairly stable and manipulable world, is

[1] Descartes, 'Concerning the nature of the human mind: that it is more easily known than the body', *Meditations on First Philosophy*.

indeed exceedingly problematic. It was Hume who showed just how very problematic it is. How different it would have been if only Descartes had been right! A luminously certain and indubitable base-line, a cognitive immaculate conception, was to be linked by a series of almost equally immaculate steps, each inheriting the reliability of the base-line, to a *safely* knowable world. This world would be the worthy object of a blemish-free, and indeed divinely underwritten cognitive process. An apostolic succession of clear and distinct ideas would replace the erstwhile apostolic links between us and the point of Revelation.

Nothing of this remains. Descartes had helped to formulate the problem. His actual solution is of historic interest only. Descartes formulated the criteria of attaining an acceptable world, criteria we in effect retain; his successors have shown that we do not and cannot satisfy them. Hume showed that the links which bind the immediate data, reliably available to the anxious individual, to the constructed and completed world, were in no way guaranteed by anything whatever. They could not, as Descartes had thought, spontaneously generate both their own starting point and the guarantee linking it with its corollaries. Examination of the data themselves could, for instance, bring up nothing corresponding to a causal nexus which links the observed with the unobserved, and induces us to believe in the reality of the latter. The only thing which impels us to connect events in terms of causation is previous experience of similar sequences. But nothing can ever guarantee their continued repetition. Nothing can lead us to reason causally, other than our contingent but well-established habit of doing so; yet without it, we cannot construct a world.

So Hume fell back on the *custom* of the mind so as to explain the manner in which it could attain or build a world. That custom itself was beyond the reach of any vindication. We can only use it – we have no choice in the matter – and hope it will not let us down. If Descartes was anguished because he could not bear the idea of God the deceiver, Hume was anguished because he could find no good reasons to trust the convictions by which we live. He had accepted the Cartesian programme, but saw the impossibility of its successful completion.

Though Hume returned to the custom which Descartes had spurned, and made it central for his account of knowledge, it cannot be said that he returned to the (as yet unnamed) notion of *culture*. Descartes, without naming it, had tried hard to free himself from it. Custom is crucial for Hume: but it is still the universal custom of a generic human mind. It is not yet, at any rate when he deals with the problem of knowledge, the specific custom of a given community. Hume's thought is in the main psychologistic, not sociologistic.

This, then, is the main difference between the two thinkers: they attempted to carry out the same programme, but one thought it feasible, and the other saw that it was nothing of the kind. But there were also some other more specific but interesting differences. For instance, what happens to Descartes's solid self, the 'thinking substance'? Hume is clear on the point:

> ...nor have we any idea of *self*...from what impression could this idea be derived?...yet 'tis a question, which must necessarily be answered, if we would have the idea of self pass for clear and intelligible. ...I may venture to affirm of...mankind, that they are nothing but a bundle or collection of different perceptions, which succeed each other with an inconceivable rapidity, and are in a perpetual flux and movement.[1]

Clarity and intelligibility, succeeding Descartes's clarity and distinctness, are turned against Descartes's conclusion. They deprive us of that hard, solid self which Descartes seemed to offer, and which was his base.

On this point, Kant seems very much in agreement with Hume:

> ...in what we entitle 'soul', everything is in continual flux and there is nothing abiding except (if we must so express ourselves)

---

[1] David Hume, *A Treatise of Human Nature*, book I, part IV, section VI (first published 1739).

the 'I', which is simple solely because its representation has no content...[1]

The hard, gem-like substantial self, so dear and important for Descartes, is gone. What is admittedly left, both in Hume and in Kant, *nur mit ein bisschen anderen Worten*, is another self, no longer a substance, but rather an activity. For Hume it is, notoriously, a *bundle*, accumulated with a suggestion of passivity on its own part. For Kant, it is the activities which assemble the world. The self is rather like what they call the 'link man' on television: it binds the separate perceptions so that they form a unity. Kant tries to chart these binding activities with meticulousness. For him, these activities really *are* the self.

The Copernican counter-revolution

Hume and Kant both inherit Descartes's problem: how can the human mind, from its own resources, arrive at a justifiable, warranted knowledge of the world? It must use its own resources, for it no longer trusts Culture or Authority. Liberation from dependence on the accidents of a given historic situation is central for Descartes, and these terms of reference are taken over by Hume and Kant. When all is said and done, they were thinkers of the Enlightenment. To transfer cognitive sovereignty to 'custom and example' would mean, in effect, to endorse any old *ancien régime*. This (though Hume was fairly conservative in politics) they could hardly wish to do.

This is the essence of the rationalist programme: it is opposed to the acceptance of the reality of the world on trust. It knows no loyalty to a culture and its custom. On the contrary, it views culture with the utmost suspicion. When Descartes shows loyalty to his Church, what characteristically attracts him to it is the

[1] Immanuel Kant, *The Critique of Pure Reason*, Paralogisms of Pure Reason (first published 1781).

centralist, unified, single source of the Revelation, its tidy tran-
scendentalism, rather than its incarnation in a *historic* tradition.
Descartes is rationalist even, or especially, in his Faith. The
rationalist, hence anti-dogmatic or anti-authoritarian stance, sees
the mind as facing the problem of knowledge of the world, without a prior commitment to (or faith in) *any* world and, *a fortiori*, to
any particular culture. It is the expression of a mind determined
to accept only rationally defensible cognitive claims, judged by
laws of reason which transcend any one culture and any one
world.

Hume and Kant are conventionally regarded as holders of rival
views, but in fact they share a very great deal. Hume's ambivalent
scepticism, and Kant's supposed answer to it, have far more in
common with each other than either has with Descartes. The
French thinker had provided them both with their problem and
with its terms of reference. The difference between Hume and
Kant is largely, though not wholly, one of tone, spirit, stress, and
terminology.

The world *we* know, or claim to know, and live in, is not just a
flux of transient impressions, a buzzing booming confusion: it is
an orderly, law-abiding, habitable and manipulable world. In the
eighteenth century, it was rapidly becoming rather more intelligible and manipulable – and manipulated – than it had ever been
before. Newton had demonstrated its intelligibility. He had
shown that it is composed of fairly solid and stable things, with
decently tidy habits, which make science – and in due course also
modern, technology-based production – possible. It is the kind of
world a cognitively and industrially respectable person is willing
to be seen in, and where he can make an honest living by
exploiting the orderly predictability of things to his own advantage. It is a world broken up into objects in a manner that enables
us to communicate and cohabit with other minds which share our
system of classification.

Naively, we often suppose that such a world is our birthright.
Descartes knew that it was nothing of the kind: but he thought
that such a world could be attained by achievement rather than
ascription. Think hard and think neatly, and it will be given unto

you. Cartesian man does not inherit his world from dad, he makes his own by hard and conscientious thought. Descartes also supposed that the attainment of such a world could be justified by the human mind *without cheating*. It could be done by the use of bona fide, non-circular steps, all at once both inwardly compelling and objectively legitimate.

Inner compulsion, though only of the proper orderly bourgeois kind of course, attaching to clear and distinct ideas, thus coverged with cognitive legitimacy. *Ordnung muss sein.* The world was fortunately so constructed that the order-revering and clarity-respecting intuitions of the new men led to a valid understanding of how things really are. *Our* spirit and reality were congruent with each other. A blessed situation!

In all this, Descartes was quite mistaken. Hume's secure place in the history of philosophy rests in considerable part on the lucidity with which he showed this to be so. None the less, we still do live in that orderly world – or rather an increasing number of people do live in our particular version of it. A few men already lived in it in Descartes's time, after Galileo, and a far greater number did so by the time of Hume and Kant, after Newton. If so many of us now inhabit such a world, and yet have none of the justifications for doing so, what should we do? Can we continue to inhabit it shamelessly, unable to show any title deeds when challenged? Both Hume and Kant were deeply uneasy about inhabiting a house whose title deeds were shown to be fraudulent.

Hume thought that *no* independent, non-circular vindication of such a world was available. All he could do, and all anyone could do, was to describe how, in fact, such a world happened to be constructed, thanks to the habitual, but contingent and un-warranted, working of our minds. We just happen to be so constructed, that we note regularities, internalize them, and expect them to continue. This built-in expectation leads us to construct the type of world which in fact we do inhabit, and which we also very successfully manipulate. But all this is more of a description than a vindication. This is all that we can have, and as far as Hume was concerned, it constituted a kind of *faute de mieux* vindication. We are bound to our world only by a common law marriage, based on customary and well-established cohabitation, and not by some divinely underwritten sacrament.

Kant's strategy of vindication was in the last analysis much the same as Hume's: it was the self, and not external reality, which was responsible for the general features of our world. Kant claimed to have initiated what he called the 'Copernican Revolution' in philosophy. By this he meant the replacement of the old attempts at finding the required vindication *in the external world*, by a determined attempt to locate it *inside the human mind itself*. Bertrand Russell, who did not greatly care for Kant, indulged in the perfectly appropriate jibe that Kant should really have called it the anti-Copernican Counter-Revolution. Copernicus had shifted the centre of the world *away* from man, away from the Earth to the Sun. Kant had done exactly the opposite. He had used philosophy to restore centrality to mankind. He made the structure of the human mind, rather than the structure of the world, pivotal and fundamental. The basic vindication of the worldly order on which we depend was to be found *inside* us, not outside.

Russell's point is perfectly valid, but there is no reason why it should be seen as a sneer. It admirably sums up the basic strategy of Kant's endeavour. It is useless to seek an external Guarantor, even though religious tradition (which Descartes replicates at this point, and which Kant thought he could save) has taught mankind to expect it. One such reason is the infinite regress which is involved. As André Gide put it in one of his novels: when you meet your Maker, how will you know He is the *real* one?

But the idea of internal validation had been anticipated by Hume. Hume's role in Kant's thought is not merely that of the great awakener of Kant from his 'dogmatic slumbers' (Kant's own phrase). Hume was not only the man who highlighted the acuteness of the problem facing Reason, if indeed it is to be responsible for the construction and legitimation of a habitable world. He also anticipated the Kantian strategy: the abandonment of the hope of demonstrating that the world must, for some reason, *be like that*. He too proposed its replacement by the somewhat more modest endeavour to show that our minds are such that we simply do not think the world in any other way. The philosophical Copernican Revolution, the shift from an appeal to the structure of the world, to an appeal to the structure of our mind, is already present in Hume.

But there still remains an important difference between the two thinkers. Kant strove to show that we *cannot* think the world differently. Hume was content with showing, rather more modestly, that we simply *do not* think it in any other way. Kant was both more demanding in what he tried to achieve, and more sophisticated concerning what it was he was doing. He would not have been content with merely describing how, as a matter of contingent and precarious fact, our minds happen to work. His inner need clearly was, as it had been for Descartes, to ensure that the foundations were sound, to *prove* that they were indeed reliable, and to make us feel safe and secure. Hume, less exigent, was also much less clear about what he was up to. He thought he was indulging in descriptive, empirical psychology, showing how the mind actually worked. To a lesser extent, in some contexts or moods, he also indulged in an account of how it *should* work, as a kind of prescriptive recommendation. He was not very clear about how these two activities of his related to each other. On these matters, Kant was rather more lucid.

Hume gives us the notion that the mind is constructed from some kind of putty or clay, on which vigorous impressions make their mark, and this is then, much more feebly, echoed by ideas. His emphatic and frequently reaffirmed principle was, in effect – *No ideas without impressions*. Hume clings to this as if his peace of mind depended on it, which it did.

Thus mental custom performs the same role, and carries the same burden, as it does in Kant's variant of world construction. But the idiom of the two thinkers, and hence the emotive suggestiveness, is very different. The metaphors or imagery in terms of which the argument of Kant's *Critique of Pure Reason* is couched are very different from those of Hume's *Treatise*, with its implied imagery of putty or clay. The mind, as presented in the great *Critique*, is described almost in terms of pulleys and levers and wheels and catches, made, one feels, in stainless steel –

flawless, clean, and above all, utterly reliable. This above all: it is utterly reliable, the product of German industry at its best. Like the finest German machinery, it will not break down. There is nothing contingent, nothing sloppy or wobbly or fortuitous about the operation of such machines. What they do, they do inexorably, reliably, *necessarily*. Order in the world is guaranteed by the precision machinery of our mind.

Kant's three great *Critiques* are the operational manuals supplied by Kant to humanity as the users of this splendid equipment. The manuals also contain advice on the detection and correction of certain habitual malfunctionings of the machinery. Past misguided philosophy was not made up of merely accidental mistakes; on the contrary, it was useful because it revealed certain built-in flaws in the design, against which humanity is obliged to be on guard. Thanks to Kant's manuals, we would from now on be well-advised about these unfortunate defects, and the corrections required when they reveal themselves in occasional operational breakdowns. The history of past and misguided philosophy was but the record of these repeated manifestations of certain inherent structural weaknesses of our mind. Like Descartes, Kant believed that we are not doomed to error: and we can avoid it if we attend carefully to his recommendations. However, for Kant the deep persistent errors are not produced by culture, but are inwardly generated by certain basic features of our intellectual equipment. Kant called this the 'dialectic', the pejorative name for a built-in temptation and inclination to a certain kind of error. So this word, soon to be used so portentously, actually entered modern philosophy as a term of denigration.

Resumé

The development which stems from Descartes can now be seen clearly. For Descartes, an inner conceptual compulsion, and it alone, provides us with the liberation from the accidental, unreliable convictions, rooted in nothing better than social precedent and pressure. A *purified* inner compulsion alone can free us from sordid submission to the historic accident of *culture*. The compulsion is inner, its grounds are transparent, and it is self-guaranteeing; but it can also engender and underwrite a whole progeny of similarly incorruptible, doubt-free convictions about the *external world*. The inner compulsion first sets the example, then provides the premiss, and finally introduces the divine Guarantor, having also supplied Him with His own credentials. Baron Munchhausen could have done no better. The world engendered in this way is knowable, reliable, and orderly.

Hume and Kant – notably Hume – examined our inner resources, and found that they simply were not up to providing a world to Descartes's specifications. Our data on their own lacked the power to supply and to guarantee with certainty the kind of world that Descartes had hoped for, and which now, thanks to Newton, was actually inhabited by Hume and Kant.

Reason had succeeded in fact, and it had failed in law. An orderly knowable world was available, but devoid of title deeds. None *could* be forthcoming. The Cartesian programme had failed, at any rate in its aspiration to provide mankind with warranty of its new and truly marvellous cognitive acquisitions. Thereby the problematic nature of Reason was laid bare. But Hume and Kant also – notably Kant – thought they could prove that the mind is so constructed that it *must* bring forth from within itself such a tidy, cognizable, Newtonian world. So we were, after all, rationally entitled to believe in it; but the considerations enabling us to do so were henceforth to be based on qualities of our mind alone.

But is the human mind identical in all ages and societies? In essence, when working out their main positions, Hume and Kant assumed that indeed it was, though contrary observations can be found in more peripheral parts of their theories. Once this was seriously questioned, the debate entered a new phase.

2
The Roots of Compulsion

The wheel comes full circle

The comparative study of diverse forms of human mentality and rationality is in large part the province of social anthropology. A thinker who, more than any other perhaps, has left his mark on the manner in which anthropology handles this issue, is Emile Durkheim.

The work of Durkheim which primarily deals with this question is *The Elementary Forms of Religious Life.*[1] In its empirical part, the book deals extensively with the ethnography of Australian aborigines. Its theoretical parts, located mainly in the early and final pages, are intimately concerned with the ideas of Hume and of Kant. This is the book in which the ethnographic investigation of diverse human rationalities, in the plural, comes up against the philosophical inquiry into generic human reason, in the singular.

Durkheim is a severe critic of the entire empiricist tradition, of which Hume was the supreme exponent. With respect to Kant, Durkheim's position is more complex: he holds Kant to be not so much incorrect as gravely incomplete. The required completion was in his view to be found in his own, Durkheim's, work.

[1] E. Durkheim, *The Elementary Forms of Religious Life: A study in religious sociology*, tr. Joseph Ward Swain (Allen and Unwin, London, 1915, repr. 1976).

The Durkheimian solution of Kant's problem at the same time also became a Charter of Ethnographic Research. According to Durkheim, Kant is right when he says that conceptual compulsion was both essential for our humanity and sprang from within our own minds. The order which makes things knowable is not inherent in those things themselves: it inheres in the manner in which our mind handles and classifies them. But Kant had failed to find out just *how* it was all instilled in us. Durkheim's answer was – *by ritual*. If this is true, the correct method for the understanding of the human mind is not by introspection, or even in the psychological laboratory, but by anthropological fieldwork. Go out and observe the social practices which instil shared conceptual compulsions in men.

Consider Durkheim's critique of the empiricists. Durkheim's charge against them is that they fail even to recognize, let alone to account for, the pervasive presence of *compulsion* in our mental life. We *cannot but* think causally, for instance. Likewise, we are deeply committed to the persistence of solid objects. The world is law-bound, it is as it were cemented into substantiality, causality, regularity in space and time. We cannot, simply *cannot*, think the world any other way. These are the particular compulsions which specially interested Kant. We also have deep moral compulsions: our fervent moral convictions also leave us with no options. They firmly hold us in their grip. Durkheim, a faithful follower of Kant in this respect, believed that our conceptual and our moral compulsions have one and the same source, though he disagrees with Kant about the nature of that single root.

The empiricists could not account for this compulsion. They have great trouble with *any* compulsion: their world is, so to speak, floppy and *loose*. It coagulates by accident, like a snowball. In the case of Hume and his followers, the structure of the world was explained in terms of 'association', a kind of clotting or clustering of perceptions, attracted to each other by various associative principles, such as similarity, or contiguity in space or time. It generates no structures, but only rather accidental *bundles*, accumulated almost at random.

In anthropology these principles reappear, under the names of sympathetic and homoeopathic magic, in James Frazer's *Golden Bough*.[1] Frazer's work constitutes the application of Hume's psychology to ethnographic material. These coagulations of perceptions, stuck together by the inherently viscous properties of the material, like the rolling snowball, make up the 'things' and all the relationships of our world. Frazer used this to show amongst other things the construction of a world pervaded by magic. A fragile base for a habitable world, whether magical or scientific, one would think. Hume noted the fragility, but thought we had to live with it. We possessed no other means of gluing the world together.

Kant's solution was not really very much more powerful. From the way he talked, you might easily obtain the impression that the mind was a beautifully designed mechanism, so constructed as to ensure the production of a world along the lines required. But stripped of its metaphorical suggestiveness, and spelt out coldly, what it all amounts to is this: *if* we are to have the kind of world which in fact we think we have, that is one with stable objects endowed with definite location, size, etc., then we are *also*, *ipso facto*, committed to 'categories' (crucial central concepts) such as causal regularity.

Without causation, for instance, there would be no way of ascribing location, size, stability, to the objects of our world. Unless the existence of *some* causal properties is assumed, there is no way of distinguishing a shrinking object from one which is merely receding into the distance: the 'perceptions' are the same. There would be no way of distinguishing a rotating observer from a rotating environment. It is merely thanks to the ascription of *some* causal properties to things that we can also assign location to them, and distinguish between *their* movement and the movement of an observer. Specific causal laws cannot be established *a priori*; but we do know *a priori* that there must be some such laws, and so we can then set about finding them. We 'know' it because we already assume a world of *objects*.

---

[1] J.G. Frazer, *The Golden Bough: A study in magic and religion*, 16 vols (3rd edn, Macmillan, London, 1913, repr. 1990).

What Kant had really established was that the very elements which enter into the construction of our orderly world come as a package deal: we cannot, for instance, abandon the notion of causation, and yet retain a world of isolable, identifiable objects. It amounts to the quasi-tautology – if this is the kind of world you have, then you will have this kind of world.

So Kant's 'solution' to the question: why is our world endowed with so compulsive an order, amounts in part to a stylistic or metaphorical trick. All this talk about the mind doing this or that, and being obliged by its structure to do so, like some system of pulleys and levers, really means that our orderly world presupposes certain principles, and that these principles cannot be shown to inhere in the nature of things. By elimination, they must inhere in *us*. And, as long as we inhabit the kind of world we do indeed inhabit, we are committed to interpreting the world in terms of those principles.

Kant does not really have any good account of what happens to us when we are drunk, feverish, under drugs, very young, or in the course of confused dreams: when our tidy and compulsive categorial apparatus is suspended or damaged or not yet properly developed. It was left to anthropologists to construct a model of the 'primitive mind' on the analogy of such states. The sheer possibility of such mental conditions highlights the problem: how do we attain order and escape confusion? Durkheim does offer a solution.

Empiricists talk as if we just *happened* to find order in the world. But we were *bound* to find it. We are compulsively drawn to a certain kind of pattern, and we would not be able to live without it. How were these compulsions arranged?

Durkheim's criticism of the empiricists or associationists could have been put even more strongly. If the coagulation of our perceptions were achieved simply by association, what on earth could prevent the pervasive occurrence of a kind of semantic cancer, of the associations spreading in all directions in a simultaneously chaotic and omnivorous manner? What indeed. 'Free association' is really a pleonasm. Association is inherently free: it can, and does, move from anything to simply *anything*.

Shakespeare had something to say about the limited power of association to mitigate pain:

> O! Who can hold a fire in his hand
> By thinking on the frosty Caucasus?
> (*Richard II*, Act I, sc. ii)

But this also shows the *un*limited power of association. Bertrand Russell confessed somewhere that his familiarity with these lines permanently committed his mind to the inverse cross-association of heat with cold. By *association*, you can get anywhere. By the time you add 'contrariety' to the association-engendering relations (as Hume actually does, in so many words), association cannot fail: heads they win, tails you lose. Association is law-less, it can establish links *anywhere*. Our concepts, by contrast, are astonishingly well-disciplined. How on earth could anarchic association engender such well-drilled concepts and produce such an orderly and stable world?

Association is boundless, unconstrained and undisciplined. It is all a bit like the claim that in London, starting from any random inhabitant, one can reach any other specified inhabitant, say the Queen or the Prime Minister or the manager of Arsenal Football Club, in two or three steps, by following only the links of acquaintance. Associations of ideas are even richer and better connected than the acquaintances of men. Anything can lead anywhere.

Whatever might happen on the psychoanalyst's couch, where free association is made obligatory, rather than being proscribed as is more commonly the case, in real life we do not think as we please. We do not associate anything with anything. We think as we *must*. Our culture thinks in us. Conceptually and verbally, we are astonishingly well-disciplined and well-behaved. Both our capacity to communicate, and the very maintenance of social order, depend on it. Associations are born free, but are everywhere in chains. Society would hardly be possible otherwise. Our interpersonal concepts are circumscribed by publicly imposed limits. Their deployment is not greatly affected by the private associations which they happen to carry for individuals. If Humeian associationist empiricism constituted an accurate account of our psychic life, this could not be so. Hence Frazer's anthropology, based on Hume's psychology, cannot be correct either. Associationist psychology and anthropology starts from an appallingly undisciplined mechanism – association – and hopes to explain astonishingly well-organized structures such as our world, our language, our society. It cannot be done.

Frazer's *Golden Bough* is a classic of anthropology which describes a world which never existed and can never exist. The formula on which that splendid book is constructed is simple. Frazer assumes, though he does not say so in so many words, that Hume's psychology is valid, that Hume's *Treatise* correctly describes the manner in which human beings form their ideas and build up their picture of the world. Frazer then proceeds to assemble an unmatched richness of ethnographic data concerning the stranger beliefs and practices of mankind, and to *explain* them by invoking the principles of psychological associationism.

The oddities of human belief are explained by invoking the indisputable truth that it is only too easy for men to make mistaken, unscientific associations. It is thus, by the misguided use of association, that Frazer accounts for the predilection of the human mind for the bizarre claims of magic. Magic is wrong virtually by definition: when men use the association of ideas correctly, what they do ceases to be magic and becomes science. Magic never prospers, for when it does, no-one dares call it magic. One calls it science instead. This Frazerian explanation, both of the misguided and of the successful use of data and its patterns, is simply too easy. Frazer can perhaps explain the oddity, but cannot explain the order and similarity of human vision. Frazer can explain our transgressions against logic; he cannot explain the manner in which our minds are drawn to *order*, whether magical or scientific, and the way in which, within any one society, order is largely shared.

Durkheim's charge against the empiricists was that they could not explain the pervasive compulsive constraints, the remarkable congruence of ideas within any one society; and indeed, that they barely noticed it. The principle of association would lead us to expect the opposite. Frazer was concerned only with social variety and the frequent absurdity, not with the discipline, of human thought. Kant recognized and described it admirably (or rather, he described the form it assumed in a Newtonian and protestant society), but he did not and could not genuinely explain it. He said, in effect, that 'the mind did it'. But what does that mean? He insisted that the mind was subject to inescapable inner compulsions, that it could not but think in a certain way: but why, and how?

So, according to Durkheim, Kant had seen the problem, which the empiricists had not really faced, but failed to supply its solution. He described the compulsion; or, to be more precise, he described one particular, historically and culturally distinct, set of compulsions, namely that of Western protestant-rationalist individualists. By what was basically a stylistic or expository device, he presented his description of it as an explanation. Moreover, at the same time, he implausibly claimed and believed, at least in his main and official view, that he was describing the universal human mind.

Durkheim offered a more genuine, and at the same time less ethnocentric account. He offered an explanation which also allowed for cultural diversity, for the fact that, although all men do indeed live under the domination of compulsive concepts, the nature of those compulsions varies a great deal from one society and period to another.

It is in this way that Durkheim brought philosophy and anthropology together. Our conceptual and moral compulsions, which alone make us human and social and which preoccupied Kant, are, he maintained, instilled in us by ritual. Ritual is not identical in all societies. But its underlying role remains the same. In the crazed frenzy of the collective dance around the totem, each individual psyche is reduced to a trembling suggest-ible jelly: the ritual then imprints the required shared ideas, the collective representations, on this malleable proto-social human matter. It thereby makes it concept-bound, constrained, and socially clubbable.

The morning after the rite, the savage wakes up with a bad hangover and a deeply internalized concept. Thus, and only thus, does ritual make us human. Animal mental life, as far as Durkheim was concerned, could be handed over to the Associationists. Animal organisms can build up patterns of expectation built on association. Hume's philosophy of mind will do for animals, but not for us. We become human by becoming Kantian. Inverting a pun of Quine's, we become human by ceasing to be Humeian. Our concepts acquire sharp boundaries, resistant to the vagaries of association, and they acquire boundaries shared by all members of a ritual community. The compulsiveness of these shared mental contents is imposed by collective ritual.

This part of Durkheim's argument is normally associated with the theory that in religion, society unwittingly worships itself, *par divinités interposées*. This doctrine is indeed to be found in his work: but it is far less interesting and important than the view that what makes us human and social is our capacity to be constrained by compulsive concepts, and the theory that the compulsion is instilled by ritual, and that ritual is the core of religion. In this sense, it was religion, and religion alone, which made us human. I do not know whether this theory is true, and I doubt whether anyone else knows either: but the question to which it offers an answer is a very real and serious one. No better theory is available to answer it. No other theory highlights the problem so well.

Mankind lives and thinks conceptually. Concepts are communally shared inner compulsions. They are linked to external tokens, and also to external conditions of deployment. Humanity is the one species which is not genetically pre-programmed in its behaviour. Its intolerably volatile potential must, within any one community, be restrained, if cohesion, cooperation and communication are to be possible at all. Collective rituals inculcate shared compulsions, thereby quite literally humanizing us. We cooperate because we think alike, and we think alike thanks to ritual. Durkheim's version of the Social Contract has the merit of not being circular. It does not *assume* rationality and social obligation among those who set up social order. It shows how those who lack either can be induced to acquire it. In this way, rituals make society possible, and in this way, they also make us human. This is the core of Durkheim's theory.

Dénouement

So the wheel has come full circle. Descartes distrusted socially induced beliefs as prejudice, and sought liberation from them through the use of inescapable inner compulsions. Durkheim accepted the empiricists' point that the actual data of our consciousness lacked any basis for such compulsion. But he insisted that we were indeed endowed and guided by compulsions, and that we could not be either social or human without them. This being so, a social anthropology using empiricist psychology as its premiss could not conceivably account for the most striking and important features of our social life – our conceptual and moral discipline, our capacity to communicate, our submission to social order.

The socially indispensable compulsions were the voice of society within us, and they were injected into us by ritual. So if Durkheim is right, Descartes, when he wished to elude social prejudice, used as his guide and saviour in the flight from the social *precisely that which is in reality the voice of society within us*! He sought escape from the daemon who would mislead us: and he found the salvation precisely in that which the daemon instils in us. Fleeing from the fiend, he threw himself into his arms. Conceptual compulsions are the work of 'custom and example', or rather, of the emphatic, formalized version of custom and example, namely ritual. Descartes blithely entrusted himself to that which he wished to elude. He found the sanctuary from the daemon in the daemon's principal stronghold.

Descartes v. Durkheim

Imagine Descartes confronted by Durkheim. No doubt Descartes would refuse to be overawed by Durkheim's theory. He might well reply to Durkheim along the following lines: in constructing my argument, I did indeed make very sure that I should not be deceived, *conned*, into conviction by any alien agency, whether it be society, which is what you, Monsieur Durkheim, claim that it is, or whether it be anything else. The precise identity of the Deceiver did not concern me too much, though the fear that it might be society and history was only too present. I deliberately invoked the supposition of an all-powerful and malignant daemon, so as to flush out any possible source of disinformation, however cunningly disguised. I refused to endorse anything insinuated by such a daemon, whoever he, she or it might be, for this very reason.

So, as you can see, your little trick of claiming that my ideas might be imposed on me by a cunning social mechanism, was not at all absent from my calculations. I allowed for it, indeed I was deeply preoccupied with it. That fear or supposition was upper-most in my mind. Far from not allowing for the possibility that social prejudice might speak to me through my inner conviction, this was *precisely* the danger which I was most eager to guard against.

Let us suppose that you are indeed right, that the malignant daemon does indeed exist, and is, as you so insistently claim, *Society*. *My* method of doubt was certainly so designed as to cover me against such an eventuality, at least as much as against any other. Or rather, it was designed above all to cope with this very danger. Why, the first thing my method of doubt would elimin-ate would be anything which owed its appeal and authority to mere ritual! My rules for the correct comportment of our mind excluded reliance both on custom and emotion. Ritual is nothing but the blend of rigid custom with emotional excess. *Quel horreur!*

As my means of escape and handrail out of the realm of doubt into the domain of certainty, I did not use *any old* compulsion, as you seem to think. I restricted myself to the use of the better class of compulsion, if you know what I mean. As my prime and shining example of such a superior compulsion, I used, if I may remind you, the argument *cogito ergo sum*. The absolute compulsion which induces us to accept *that* argument, or if you like, the repulsion we feel for denying it, is well beyond the power of any ritual, whether to instil or to subvert! That is precisely why I chose it. That is just why it deserves to be the base of my edifice. It is ritual-proof. So there.

At this point, Descartes could easily pass over to the counter-attack. My dear Emile, he could add smilingly, you claim that the deep compulsions which organize our thought and life are but the fruits of ritual. They can be nothing else, you say. Ritual endows us with those constraints which organize our conceptual, moral and social lives, which bestow order on our world and our society, you claim. In that case, please try to show me, if you dare, the ritual occasion to which, on your account, I must have been subjected, and as a consequence of which I became so deeply committed to the link between my *thought* and my *existence*. Presumably it was done in the course of some nameless orgy! Only a most potent ritual could induce such a deep and irresistible conceptual compulsion. But I assure you, the sober Jesuits who trained me at La Flèche, though of course they practised the Catholic rites, at no time reduced me to trembling ecstasy by hopping up and down whilst chanting *cogito sum, cogito sum, cogito sum*! The Rector, Father Charlet, would never have allowed any such thing. Anyone indulging in such a practice would have been expelled *at once*, without mercy. So the very thing which, on your own account, could alone ever explain my deeply internalized and irresistible subjection to the truth of the *cogito*, never actually happened! There you have an *experimentum crucis*, if ever there was one. Your famous theory of the social and ritual origin of inner conceptual compulsion must now be seen for what it is: an indefensible and irrevocably refuted error. It was an interesting and ingenious theory, and as such is to your credit, but we now clearly see that it is false.

It must be conceded that Descartes's hypothetical riposte to Durkheim is powerful. Can Durkheim's theory be saved? Can Durkheim answer Descartes? If you wish to know the answer turn to the next section.

Selective compulsion, or Durkheim and Weber[1]

Durkheim in all probability cannot defend himself against Descartes's counter-charge on his own. Without any shadow of doubt, Descartes did experience an acute conceptual compulsion, and yet it was totally unrelated to any collective ecstatic ritual. It was intended to defy the voice of collectivities and the suggestiveness of rites, and it owed nothing to them. In fact, he attained his conviction in quiet solitude, indulging in reflection and meditation. He reached his compulsion whilst sitting by a peasant stove, in the midst of a lull in the Thirty Years' War. His intense and compulsive conviction was directed against rituals; it was not their voice.

But a riposte is available. Durkheim would be able to formulate it, but only if he availed himself of intellectual support by a contemporary with whom he did not in fact significantly interact: Max Weber.[2]

Durkheim's theory of concept formation amounts to the claim that they arise by controlled and collective social imposition. This theory is meant to explain why *all* men are rational: why all men think in severely circumscribed, shared and demanding concepts, rather than in terms of privately assembled and perhaps wildly diverging associations. This is what Durkheim means by

[1] My exposition of Durkheim and Weber focuses on certain themes in their thought which are important for my argument. It does not present all aspects of their ideas in the round, so to speak. For a more complete exposition, see for instance S. Lukes, *Emile Durkheim: His life and work* (Harper and Row, New York and London, 1973); A. Giddens, *Durkheim*, Fontana, London, 1978; R. Brubaker, *The Limits of Rationality: An essay on the social and moral thought of Max Weber* (Allen and Unwin, London, 1984); W. Schluchter, *The Rise of Western Rationalism: Max Weber's developmental history*, tr. Guenther Roth (University of California Press, Berkeley and London, 1981).

[2] cf. Max Weber, *The Protestant Ethic and the Spirit of Capitalism*, tr. Talcott Parsons (Unwin University Books, London, 1930, repr. 1965). Those who wish to consider further the question as to whether Weber and Durkheim knew of each other and interacted at all should consult E.E. Tiryakian, 'A problem in the sociology of knowledge: the mutual unawareness of Emile Durkheim and Max Weber', *European Journal of Sociology*, 7.2 (1960).

rationality. It explains why men think under compulsion, and why the compulsions are *shared* in any one cultural community, though not by all mankind.

This theory, however, does not differentiate between one system of shared compulsions and another. It explains them all, and does not on its own commend any one of them above the others. Like the rain which falls gently on the just and the unjust, it applies to all human cultures, favouring none.

But suppose that this theory were to be complemented by another, and one concerned to show, not why all men are rational, but why *some men are more rational than others*. Such an elevation of some men over others does not make much sense in terms of Durkheim's original theory: all men think in terms of concepts. So, as far as that goes, all men are rational. But in another sense, rationality is not quite so evenly distributed.

Assume a community of men, rational in Durkheim's primary sense, and exemplifying his theories: the community subdivides into groups, whose diverse statuses are ritually confirmed, and hence are very deeply internalized. The same is true of the temporal rhythm of their lives. The meanings they communicate, and the obligations they recognize, are deeply incorporated into their ideas, and these are instilled into them by the solemnity of their collective rites. Participation in the rites is not merely a condition of membership of the community and of its segments: it is also a way, and the only way, of learning and internalizing the expectations, the rights and duties, which make a man what he is, which endow him both with his generic humanity and his specific social niche. The ideas by which men live are hier-archically ordered: important ideas are endowed with big and dramatic rites, and lesser notions are not favoured with quite so much emphasis. Such is humanity *à la* Durkheim.

But suppose now that for some reason, this community becomes part of a wider one, which contains the cult of a High God. This deity happens to be a jealous deity. Its priests and doctrines seek and proclaim exclusive worship of Him alone. In the course of the rivalry between the literate priests of the central and exclusive cult, and the more ecstatic ritual practitioners of minor and locally rooted ones, the adherents of the central and jealous faith also abjure and condemn magic. The manipulation of things for personal advantage is reprobated. They favour the observance of moral rules rather than the purchase of advantage, whether through magical manipulation or through the propitiation of spirits or prestations. They favour a transcendent which imposes a moral and/or natural order, rather than one which presents the supernatural as just one further flexible and bribable patronage system, within which support and protection are exchanged for adherence, gifts and submission.

Such a faith may, rather unusually, stress morality and rule-abidingness at the expense of magic, patronage, and loyalty. It commends upright consistency more than submission. Its ritual style acquires a new emphasis: it refrains from excessive stress on the special occasion, and endeavours as far as possible to extend ritual solemnity to *all* aspects of life. It may for instance repudiate the use of oaths, and claim that all affirmations without exception should be equally solemn and trustworthy. It may go a long way towards levelling out ritual, thus ensuring that even daily activities partake of ritual solemnity. All life becomes solemn and rule-bound, all affirmations are treated with respect, and all men come eventually to partake of priesthood. Such a style may indeed in the end come close to levelling out the differentiation between priesthood and laity, in effect turning *all* believers into priests, with none being more priestly than others.

This centralized faith is also scriptural, and uses writing extensively, endowing it with sacredness. Context-free written statements treat all men alike; hence scripturalism has a certain natural affinity with spiritual egalitarianism. Spoken words owe their impact to context or emphasis, but a written revelation is neutral, for it cannot easily discriminate amongst diverse potential readers. The use of writing by the clerisy leads it to shift gradually from narrative to theory: legal prescriptions, more than exemplary stories, convey the shared meanings and obligations to the faithful. This explicitness encourages systematization and theoretical justification; rivalry of theories engenders doctrinal strife and a more precise formulation of the faith, and so leads to the idea of heresy. Orthopraxy and its precondition, ortho-conceptualization, are complemented, and even in part replaced, by orthodoxy. Rules become more important than loyalty, and faith more crucial than works. Works were stressed when a specialized religious organization encouraged the faithful to offer prestations or corvée to divinities, temple, or monastery. A community of equal believers prefers its members to observe rules, rather than to come bringing gifts. Inner sanctions become more powerful than outer ones. Compulsions are freed from a dependence on external stimulus, in other words, on ritual emphasis.

Assume further, that this symmetrical ethos, with its level and even diffusion of the sacred, now focused on one ineffably distant deity, comes to be practised in a new kind of socio-political milieu: one in which commercial relations have become very widespread, where the division of labour is rather well developed, and where the political order is strongly established, and is based on a rule of law rather than on patronage. In such a society, political caution and economic advantage no longer impel men quite so strongly towards the formation of social subgroupings. Fidelity to contract becomes more important than loyalty to clan or chief. In both their economic and political dealing, men are allowed or even encouraged to adopt a certain individualism, an ethic of rule-observance, of the like treatment of like cases. Both people and things are treated in a more orderly way. Contract prevails over status. Status may best be internalized by means of intermittent and heavily emphatic ritual; but respect for all contracts is more likely to be instilled by a well-diffused, even-tempered, sustained seriousness and quiet reverence. So the celebrated move from status to contract may well go with a shift from ritual to conscience, from external theatre to the inner voice.

In such a social order, the sacred is still that which endows us with our compulsions, as Durkheim taught. But it is now a radically different kind of compulsion: it works differently and attaches itself to a different kind of object. The sacred no longer endorses this or that crucial concept; rather, it instils respect for certain formal properties of *all* concepts. It is evenly spread out, rather than concentrated in specially sacred times and places.

Hence it no longer sacralizes specific institutions, but rather an orderly, symmetrical, rule-bound general manner of proceeding and thinking. It is orderliness, respectability, organization in a tidy system, which is endowed with an aura of authority, and which become compulsive in the minds of men. All life is socialized; sobriety replaces ecstasy as *the* religious condition; absence of symbols becomes the token of faith. The orderliness extends to the vision of nature. Curiosity about nature is less likely to seek the short cut and privilege of revelation, a kind of privileged cognitive favour, and more likely to use *investigation*, which expects and seeks no favours.

Possibly the theory-addiction of this kind of society has led some of its theoreticians to work out the implications of their beliefs. The exclusive deity is declared to be all-powerful and all-knowing. That the wicked will suffer eternal punishment after death has long been part of the creed and its sanction. The terrifying joint implication of these two ideas, of predestination and punishment, is well known: some men are predestined, even before they are born, for eternal torment. Salvation and damnation must have been willed and distributed by the deity from the very start.

Members of this tradition, especially if their daily employment permits or encourages reflection, have pondered their situation. They worry about the future of their souls as well as of their investments, or rather more so. They are much given to reflection on their condition: both their life-style and their faith encourage reflection, moral stocktaking. Their anxiety about their peril is ever latent, and often very acute and tormenting. What can they do?

The only strategy available to them is to look out for signs of their own Election. They cannot logically *bring it about*, for the die has been cast long ago. They cannot purchase it by manipulation or propitiation. Their ethos discourages attempts at bribing the divine; their sense of order precludes it; the dismantling of spiritual hierarchy deprives them of the mediators who could have solaced and reassured them and would have received the appropriate prestations. They are dreadfully alone in their anxiety.

Suppose they are also told that they are not expected to indulge in special ritual activity, but that the best sign of their election is the sober and successful performance of their worldly calling. All callings are equally sacred. They will throw themselves into their work, not because worldly success as such means much to them, still less because they would allow themselves to enjoy its fruits, but because it is the only way in which they can in some measure allay their own dreadful inner fear. The irony is that economically disinterested commitment to work is the very best recipe for economic success. A *calculating* devotion to honesty would lapse whenever expedient, in other words pretty often, and be at the mercy of the doubtful expectation that *others* will be similarly honest. Such an expectation is seldom well-justified: so no one will initiate the rush into honesty, for he who would be the first to do so would in all probability suffer. Others would not follow his example, but simply exploit his naivety.

But members of our new sect would pioneer the advance into probity, not from calculation, which could seldom be justified and persuasive, but rather as a side-effect of their inner spiritual torment. Hence they will not be concerned with the possibility that others may fail to follow them. They do not care. They are not in it for the money, they are not concerned with reciprocity, and they are not deterred by the consideration that honest work is not rewarded in a coercion-oriented social order, populated by others not similarly motivated. They are in it to allay an inner fear.

If sufficiently numerous and determined, these men may well transform the moral climate, and eventually induce others to follow them. Once the attitude is widespread, it will eventually become rational to emulate it. The hump has been passed. The initial uncalculating and hence reliable probity may encourage others to follow suit. The unbreakable deadlock, which normally inhibits the establishment of a rule-abiding, cooperative and efficiently productive society – it pays no-one to be the first to be good, when others are still opportunistic – is at long last broken! In a moral climate of mutual trust, enterprise prospers.

The most famous aspect of this theory is that it offers an explanation of the emergence of a successful and dominant commercial, and eventually industrial, society. Just as Durkheim's version of the Social Contract escaped the circularity of requiring men *already* capable of commitment to obligation, so Weber's theory of the emergence of economic rationality escapes the circularity of assuming the prior existence of men committed to the ethos of production. The appearance of such a society only presupposes that a significant group of people would work hard and soberly, without concern with reward, guided only by an inner sanction. Its members would not turn their profit into pleasure or power in this world, or salvation in the next, but carry on working disinterestedly and would reinvest, rather than turn it into status, power, and enjoyment. Such an attitude would also permit and encourage the power-holders in the society not to take pre-emptive measures against these puritanical *nouveaux riches*: they could be trusted not to use their well-gotten wealth to acquire power, and so to displace the old rulers. The old rulers might in such circumstances decide to marry into the new class rather than suppress it, and prefer to acquire their wealth as dowry rather than as confiscation.

From the viewpoint of those first engaging in it, there was nothing in the least rational about capitalist activity: on past form, the fruits of industrial labour were destined to be taken away from them by those endowed with political power. This did not, however, bother puritan entrepreneurs, for they had turned to the new economic ethic not in the hope of wealth, but only in the surreptitious hope of finding evidence for their own salvation.

It was really quite irrational to behave in this kind of way. There was nothing rational about rationality. On past evidence no good could ever come of it, from a worldly viewpoint. In the event, it did pay off, but there was no way of foreseeing this. So, Reason was born from Unreason. Some men had been tricked into rationality: and because they were numerous enough, and the circumstances were propitious, eventually, and somewhat to their own surprise, they greatly prospered. As Wesley noted, religiosity led to prosperity, which was in the end liable to subvert it. But had affluence been their initial aim and concern, they could never have taken the path which ultimately led to great wealth. They gained wealth because they did *not* pursue it. It was necessary to forsake the lust for gain, if gain was to be secured on a truly phenomenal, historically quite unprecedented scale. You must forsake the world if you are to gain it.

The implications of Weber's famous theory for economic history does not at the moment concern us directly. We are concerned with what this religious style does for rationality itself. What it achieves is that the solemnity, that is linked in a Durkheimian world to ecstasy, to the *special* occasion, to the stratification of obligations and identities, to the sacralization of *some* practices and ideas, now attaches itself instead, in a pervasive and commanding manner, to sobriety, and to all the details of ordinary life, in a symmetrical and unselective way. Abstention from ritual itself becomes the most potent ritual; the absence of graven images becomes the most powerful fetish. The rules of symmetrical evidence, of orderly criteria for assessing ideas and data – the very opposite of the authority of heightened excitement and of the localized, incarnate sacred – themselves acquire a special kind of sacred authority. The special occasion is replaced by the view that all occasions are equally sacred; the special Mediator with the Divine, by the view that all men alike are priests; and the special status of the sacred, by the view that all things partake of the sacred, and no exceptions are to be made, whether in conduct or in cognition. Nothing *in the world* is more sacred than anything else: this allows or encourages the free choice of means, and so the de-sacralization of economic, investigative and other procedures. It loosens up the rigidity of tradition and its practices. Thus it opens up the possibility of innovation in cognition and production. Sacredness adheres to a formal order, not to selected items within the world. This facilitates trust and rational planning.

Descartes was not, technically speaking, a Protestant. He was and remained a loyal son of the Catholic Church. He admired its elegant centralization, and, characteristically and consistently, considered this to be one of its great merits. But every rule of intellectual comportment which he so meticulously commended, and which he so seriously strove to implement, exhibits those virtues of orderliness, sobriety, separation of issues (which is but an aspect of the division of labour), conscientiousness, which sociologists have identified as Protestant virtues.

We do not know the Weberian theory to be true, any more than we know Durkheim's theory to be true. We may well never know, in either case. But assume it to be true for a moment.

If such it is, Descartes's imaginary retort to Durkheim ceases to be unanswerable. It is of course perfectly true that the Jesuits at La Flèche never chanted *cogito sum, cogito sum* to an ecstatically intoxicated young René Descartes, sending him out into the world for ever enslaved to this idea. Hence any over-literal, simple-minded Durkheimian theory of the roots of inner *logical* compulsion would indeed be very hard or impossible to defend. The compulsive ideas of modern Cartesian man are not linked, in any one-to-one manner, to any *specific* ritual. His compulsions attach not to content, not to specific ideas, but to certain *formal* properties of ideas, which is socially induced in a more complex way. He feels compelled to submit ideas to symmetrical treatment: *that* is his real compulsion. So, a more sophisticated, Webero-Durkheimian variant of the original theory might still be worth elaborating. It could run as follows:

The acceptance of the cogito is a submission to compulsions requiring orderly, symmetrical thoughts, compulsive for anyone, any time, without the benefit of collective, induced excitement. If doubt is an instance of thought, and thought is the self, then the existence of doubt entails the self. The doubt itself in this case refutes the doubt. This compulsion works without music, incense, mummery or fancy dress. It is the acceptance of such logical compulsion which a late, sophisticated, and complex form of crypto-ritual instils in those who are under its sway. What a doctrinal, symmetrical, severely centralized and puritanically orderly religion has done is to confer the aura of sacredness on the *formal* properties of a whole system of thought. Descartes merely spelt out the idea that *nothing other than* such formal, symmetrical compulsion is authoritative. This is what Pascal could not forgive him.

A new, sophisticated mechanism of instilling compulsion has injected a new kind of compulsion into us: to accept only conclusions imposed in a state of sobriety whilst contemplating lucid, distinct, uncontentious notions. Descartes codified this new kind of compulsion; but this does not mean that it lacked social roots. It had social roots of a distinct and unusual kind. It took Weber's insight to tell us what they might be. Their roots were a complex, subtle variant of those proposed by Durkheim; but they were social roots for all that.

It is this special mutation of the sacred which impelled Descartes to seek symmetrical, generally valid reasons for conviction, so as to replace the old reliance on the local, unsymmetrical accidents of history, on the arbitrary specific rituals of this or that culture. It is this need which made him seek out a new foundation, which he endowed with a universal, symmetrical, and ineluctable authority.

So the imaginary riposte with which we have credited Descartes has not really refuted all the sociologists. It has only obliged them to adopt a Weberian elaboration of Durkheim. They do have an answer. Durkheim on his own was incapable of providing it. A Weberian refinement was required, before one could offer anything like a plausible reply. The even-toned *diffused* ritual of sober orderly living instils symmetrical rules, rather than the unsymmetrical and dramatic markers of savage communal religion.

All this helps us relate Descartes and his rationalism to the two great sociological traditions. Descartes's strategy for eluding culture, stepping outside and building his own new culture-independent world, contained two separate and distinct elements: compulsion *and* selectiveness. He was fastidious about the *kind* of inner compulsiveness to which he would entrust his convictions. Inner compulsion was his saviour, but he only respected the kind of compulsion engendered by orderly thought. Compulsions deserved to be heeded, but only if produced by thought which had separated all separable elements, and which remained compulsive irrespective of mood. The compulsion was not linked to special excitement, but on the contrary distrusted and repudiated it. It had to retain its power even when, or rather, *especially* when excitement, ecstasy, external theatrical *régie*, were wholly absent. Sobriety is the excitement of the puritan.

The two great sociologists are concerned with the two distinct elements in Descartes's thought. Durkheim is the sociologist of conceptual thought, of compulsiveness, *in general*. Weber deals with the *selective* part: with that rather special kind of compulsiveness which attaches itself only to what Descartes would recognize as the sole sound foundation of his newly found world- and thought-orderliness. Durkheim tackled the problem of why all men were rational, and Weber the problem of why some were more rational than others. Weber strove to explain the emergence of this new and most unusual and distinctive style of religious compulsiveness. He tried to show how it was induced and transmitted and instilled: not by overt and discontinuous and special ecstasy, but by the at least equally potent, though quiet and orderly, inner tension. That was Weber's specialty. He was eager to explore how a special and unique kind of rationality could emerge from the older generic rationality. Durkheimian rationality is in effect equivalent to the existence of all conceptual and communal thought. Weber is concerned with but one very special version of it. Durkheim located Reason under savage Unreason; Weber identified Unreason under modern Reason.

Each of these sociologists turns religion into the main agency for endowing man with reason. For Durkheim, religion is basically ritual, and ritual serves to confer on men those compulsively shared concepts without which they could be neither human nor social. Max Weber, operating with a far narrower or more specific notion of rationality, credits one particular religious tradition with the capacity to escape from the general Durkheimian rationality, and to transform it into something new. This does not free men from compulsion, but transforms and elevates and diffuses its nature. It causes compulsion to attach itself to formal order: and the consequence turns out to be a tremendous enhancement of human cognitive and productive power.

In the light of all this, what is one to make of the Cartesian aspiration to escape all culture, all custom and example, and reach out to a socially untainted pure Reason? It was an illusion; or at any rate, it was an illusion in part. Descartes did not escape culture. He unwittingly helped codify one highly distinctive and indeed unique culture, one pervaded by reason in an altogether new manner. It also turned out to be the basis of a new civilization. Its compulsions still have a social base, but it is a new kind of base.

A rational mind in a rational world

Where does this leave us? Suppose that Durkheim and Weber are both right: the compulsion of shared concepts is socially induced. The particular, distinctive modern kind of compulsion, a vision of a symmetrical, unified and emotively disinfected, sanitized world, is engendered by a special historic experience. We happen to be its beneficiaries and/or victims. It does not commit us to any particular and specific set of concepts; it commits us to a sober and symmetrical and so to speak unificatory treatment of whatever notions we handle. Does it follow that the authority and distinctiveness of Reason is an illusion? Is it but the ventriloquist's dummy of a given social order? Should we be relativists? Should we exclude the possibility of the attainment of a transcendent and independent truth, which Reason had promised to deliver?

I think not. Certainly, in its extreme and literal form, the Cartesian hope of individual, self-sufficient attainment of wholly independent truth, is absurd. We cannot step outside our skins, or outside our social world. We cannot think without a biological and a social infrastructure, which in turn, however, must impose its limits on what or how we think. We cannot liberate ourselves from the constraints imposed on us by our nature. Cosmic exile is indeed an illusion.

Nonetheless, the *coupure* or discontinuity which Descartes and the rationalists codified is a very real one. Something new happened with the coming and dominance of sober Reason. Cosmic exile is an illusion, but exile from culture, or rather, from the whole class of cosy pre-scientific cultures, is not. Cosmic exile was a fitting philosophical myth, accompanying, ratifying and explaining the transition to a new rationality. The world in which Reason has come to assume the place which it now enjoys is profoundly distinct from the world which preceded it. Reason is not free of earthly roots, as Descartes had hoped, but it has its own distinctive ones.

What, in simple and general terms, are the characteristics of Reason and of the world it dominates? Reason is, twice over, universalistic. It is a generic faculty incarnate and latent in all men, even if its operation is on many occasions inhibited. The cognitive style is more or less correctly codified by the rationalists, requiring all concepts to observe the same rules in relation to evidence, and subject to its evidence, which in turn is not controlled by culture but in large measure free of it and is not in any way genetically restricted, though most cultures fail to promote it. The assumption that there is such a faculty is tantamount to the denial of privileged Knowers. Privileged location or incarnation of knowledge, in other-world Revelation, is similarly excluded. The assumption that such a faculty exists amounts to the claim that all cognitive claims are equal, and subject to criteria which can in principle be applied by anyone. In this sense, reason is latent in us all.

This potential symmetry or equality of all inquirers also applies to the *objects* of all investigation. The world is assumed to be a single system, governed by the same laws (even if we do not know what they are). The world as a whole, or the manner in which it is known, may be sacred, but there is no unsymmetrical, localized, privileged Sacred *within* it. The denial of both cognitive and ontological privilege is implicit in the notion of Reason. There is a deep levelling quality about Reason: it does not allow any persons or objects in the world to be very special.

Reason also possesses an inherently monopolistic tendency, and cannot in the end tolerate rivals. Hume defined Reason well:

Our reason must be considered as a kind of cause, of which truth is the natural effect...[1]

[1] David Hume, *A Treatise of Human Nature*, Bk I, Part IV, section 1.

Pascal complained of what Descartes had done:

> Je ne puis pardonner à Descartes; il aurait bien voulu…pouvoir se passer de Dieu…[1]

Socially speaking, numerous compromises, allowing peaceful coexistence between Reason and either residual, or newly invented, claims to cognitive exemption and special status, do of course exist. But Pascal's complaint, and repudiation of the 'excess' of admitting Reason alone[2] are pointless. Reason, like the deity whom she replaced (and to which she is, presumably, historically indebted) is inherently a jealous and exclusive mistress. It is this exclusive uniqueness which has led to genuine knowledge; it was the plurality of criteria which led to stagnation. In the serious cognitive life of mankind, she has indeed now acquired a powerful dominance, even if she does not succeed in eliminating the old Baalim altogether.

All these rather strong claims are made in a so-to-speak detached, descriptive, aseptic, unprejudiced spirit: this is how she appears amongst us and how she disports herself. These descriptions of her claims are made by us without endorsement, or any denial that grave problems arise for any non-circular demonstration of such claims.

In his analysis of love, Stendhal observed that it was necessary to be dry, *sec*:

> Je fais tous les efforts possibles pour être *sec*.[3]

Reason is at least as emotive a topic as love. In discussing her claims, we too must try to avoid lyrical prose. We shall endeavour to describe her, as much as possible, in a totally dry manner.

---

[1] Blaise Pascal, *Pensées* (first published 1670), vol. II.
[2] ibid., vol. IV.
[3] Stendhal, *De l'amour* (Le Divan, Paris, 1927), ch. IX.

3
The Confrontations of Reason

Introduction

Our account so far has taken the form of a narrative. With Descartes, Reason appears as a method, and in effect as the *only* method, of procuring truth. At the same time, Reason is a means of escaping those dread enemies of truth, *custom and example*. It brings liberation from mere non-rigorous and hence error-prone, error-perpetuating accretion and accumulation of ideas, from an unfastidious involvement *in*, and corruption *by*, the world; in brief, from indulgence in mere culture, a set of ideas that is contingent and bound to specific communities and periods. Reason is *purification*. By contrast, culture is corruption-on-earth. Rationality as such cannot fail: if it fails, it can only be because some impurities have been allowed to remain.

The philosophical tradition which took over Descartes's programme found that the supposedly liberating rational compulsions could not themselves in turn be validated. They could not meet their own standards, and so failed to deliver what Descartes required, namely a rational, cognizable, and above all, a guaranteed and cognitively self-justifying world. Truth was to be the touchstone both of error and of itself, as the Cartesian Spinoza put it: but such a self-validating revelation, i.e. Reason, was not to be had. The rational compulsion, no longer seen as self-generated and self-justifying, was now credited to the mechanisms of the human mind (by Hume and Kant). The mind was programmed to function in this way, but is an inner programme a proof? Later, with the coming of the proper recognition that human selves varied a good deal from culture to culture, it was also credited to history or society. They spoke to individual men through the compulsions and intuitions of entire epochs or cultures.

So the wheel had gone full circle: the daemon whom Descartes wished to escape turns up at the end of the story as the saviour; or at any rate, as the victor. Logical compulsions had social and historical roots, rather than providing an escape from history and society.

Such is the story, so far. It is a simplified, though not I hope an inaccurate account of one recent flow of thought. Additional complication and sub-plots, variations, need eventually to be added. But first the narrative must be suspended for a while.

Stepping outside the historical context for a while, it is well to attempt to describe Reason as currently conceived.

Reason is primarily a generic truth-securing faculty. As such, it is variously opposed to:

1   tradition
2   authority
3   experience
4   emotion
5   piecemeal trial and error procedure.

The biggest unquestioned assumption in the account so far is the very existence of a *generic faculty*, or alternatively, of a general criterion of truth. It is not in any way self-evident that there must be any such *single* faculty or criterion.

Imagine an alternative situation: suppose that the diverse activities, including linguistic ones, in which men indulge, were indeed quite distinct, and that these simply did not possess some single common aim or criterion. Of course, *within* each activity there might well be a right and a wrong way of going about things, there indeed would be criteria of success and failure. But the criteria in diverse fields simply would not be susceptible to any kind of summation or summary by a single principle or test or touchstone. No one method would lead to success in all spheres. Such a world is conceivable. At least one highly influential philosopher has not merely conceived it, but claimed it to correspond to the style of thought we actually practise.[1] David Hume had also considered this possibility, but he rejected it.

The contrary assumption of a generic faculty or criterion is prominent in most forms of rationalism. It is the same kind of reason that is applied to all cases, and which is identically present in all minds. Reason is impartial and universal and not tied to local circumstance. Impartiality and symmetry is of its essence. *That* is the crucial assumption. Idiosyncratic or capricious rationality, on such a view, is a contradiction in terms.

The existence of such a generic reason is often simply assumed: the debate is mainly carried on concerning the competing claims of this faculty and its rivals. Yet its sheer existence is not self-evident: our historical sketch was meant to illuminate a possible manner of its emergence. It is in this sense that Rationalism looks as if it might be the offspring of monotheism: a single and exclusive deity led us to the notion of a unique and homogeneous fount of truth. Jealous Jehovah taught mankind the Principle of Excluded Middle. Once deeply internalized, the idea becomes detached from its theological root.

For the moment, however, let us simply assume the existence of the generic faculty: and consider its various and distinct opponents.

1   Reason v. Tradition

There are two ways in which objects of all kinds, from buildings to convictions, come into being by human agency. They can be clearly planned and designed, often with a single or at least a clearly specified aim in view, and then implemented. Alternatively, they can slowly grow and emerge, serving multiple, and only obscurely perceived and formulated, ends.

---

[1] L. Wittgenstein, *Philosophical Investigations*, tr. G.E.M. Anscombe (Blackwell, Oxford, 1968).

This contrast is conspicuous, for instance, in legal and political systems and in urban architecture. Customary law stands opposed to systematic and designed statute law, Roman law to Common law, cities that have slowly grown over centuries contrast with the points of a unified urban plan. Descartes's position on this issue is plain. He is very much on the side of the single designers, and hostile to the romantics, with their strong penchant for the idiosyncratic and the 'organic'. In his day they were not yet known by any such name.

2   Reason against Authority

It is this issue which is most familiar to the general public.

It is this issue which is the one most commonly associated with Rationalism. Descartes was also very much of a rationalist in the first, anti-traditionalist sense: he approved of the deity more for its centralized procedure than for its authority. But it was in the light of his implied opposition to *authority* that he was seen by men such as Pascal.

In the end, perhaps, in their maintenance of unsymmetrical claims, Tradition and Authority do indeed stand in joint opposition to Reason. Modern Rationalism has on occasion driven them to make common cause, to become allies. As de Maistre observed, popular superstition constitutes the outer bulwarks of faith. This implies that the orderly central citadel of Revelation is in peril if deprived of those outer defences. (This seems true of Christianity, but not of Islam, where the central citadel seems strengthened by its recent disavowal and repudiation of folk accretions.) Nonetheless, neat centralized Authority is ever in latent conflict with untidy folk credulity.

Tradition opposes rationality on behalf of custom, Authority does so on behalf of a special but also possibly unique Source of Revelation. Historically, Authority and Tradition were also frequently opposed to each other. The authority-based centralized theology was often locked in conflict with the many pluralist promptings of local custom and tradition. In combating them, it prepared the ground for modern rationalism.

Nevertheless, the really big battle with which the wider public is familiar is one which pits Reason against Authority, with Tradition usually acting as a subsidiary, and sometimes important, ally of Authority. The picture contrasts the man who in the end respects only his own reason, who heeds only the evidence and rational conviction available to him, with the man who defers to Authority and Tradition. But there are also traditionalists-sceptics, men who embrace tradition because they despair of reason and prefer contingent, baseless stability to flux and uncertainty.

By rationalist terms of reference, respect for authority is blatantly circular: *if* you have good reasons for believing the Authority to be genuine, you may of course legitimately respect that Authority – but the real source of authority are the reasons which justify it, and not the authority as such. Only reasons, and not authority, can be, so to speak, terminal. But if you have no good reason, is your respect anything other than caprice?

For the Authoritarians, the rival stance seems presumptuous, impious and arrogant. How dare puny man pit his imperfect and limited reason against higher Authority? This is how J.H. Newman speaks of liberals within religion:

> There may be, and doubtless is, in the hearts of some or many of them, a real antipathy or anger against revealed truth, which it is distressing to think of.[1]

The circularity of the Authoritarian position, so repellent to us liberals, can also be invoked on its behalf and in its favour. It has a certain logic. It is plausible to argue along precisely these lines. If a defence of Faith were possible and successful, it would no longer be Faith. The reasons, if cogent, would suffice. Hence it is the nature of faith that it simply must be taken as self-justifying, i.e. accepted in a strict authoritarian spirit. 'The Judge is the Saviour.'[2] If this be so, there can be no judge concerning the validity of claims to being the saviour. The two roles have been

[1] J.H. Newman, *Apologia pro Vita Sua* (Longmans, London, 1865).
[2] K. Barth, *A Shorter Commentary on Romans* (SCM Press, London, 1959), p. 22.

fused. Paraphrasing what Spinoza said about truth, the saviour is the touchstone of both salvation and of spurious claims. The essence of rationalism, by contrast, is the *separation* of procedural and substantive legitimacy.

Logically, the fundamentalist position is impeccable. If Faith and Authority are to be allowed at all, they cannot also with any consistency either need, or allow, any rational defence. To invoke Reason is to surrender sovereignty, even if Reason should be favourable. In practice, those to whom this argument is presented might well be worried by the fact that it endorses not only one but any and every Faith, any self-appointed Authority, without discrimination. It offers protective cover to an infinity of faiths. If we lived in a world in which a single Faith confronted a single reason, the point might have some persuasiveness. (Psychologically speaking, some of the early anti-rationalists did indeed inhabit just such a world.) But we inhabit a world in which a countless number of actual and possible faiths confront Reason, which may or may not be unique.

Furthermore, formally cogent though the fundamentalist point may be, actual historic religions have not always paid much heed to it. However much they may have appealed to Faith and Authority, they also invoked reason as an additional prop. Once having allowed it in, of course, they may then have had some difficulty in circumscribing its use.

The general public is also familiar with a conflict between reason and, on the other side, not so much a privileged Authority, but special forces, magical or whatever, which are supposed to elude conventional explanation or investigation or both, and in that sense to defy Reason. Adherents or even open-minded investigators of a large number of phenomena, from astrology to metal-bending and faith-healing, are widely held to be locked in conflict with rationalism.[1]

Here the situation is rather peculiar, and frequently misunderstood by the participants themselves. It is of course perfectly

[1] W.E.H. Lecky, *History of the Rise and Influence of the Spirit of Rationalism in Europe* (Longmans, Green, London, 1910).

possible – indeed, highly probable – that the world contains forces or mechanisms which are not covered by existing scientific theories, or are actually incompatible with them. It is also possible that some of these forces have manifested themselves in phenomena classed as magical or supernatural in the past. But at this point in the argument, two possibilities arise. One is that these phenomena or forces are subjected to the normal conventions of rational inquiry: all investigators are equal, evidence is broken up into its constituent parts, circularity of reasoning is excluded, theories are tested by procedures and against data which are not under their own control, and no phenomenon is allowed to claim special status and dictate the methods of investigation into its claims. If the phenomena and their explanations survive such a scrutiny – well and good, we have enriched the corpus of our rational knowledge.

The alternative, however, is that the adepts or adherents of the special mystical force use the surprising nature of its manifestations not merely to challenge existing theories – a perfectly legitimate and rational procedure – but *also* to claim exemption, for the phenomenon or for the privileged practitioner, from ordinary methods of testing and scrutiny. This is the form in which magical and mystical phenomena actually make their social appearance: they are not merely startling in their defiance of 'normal' patterns of events, they are also accompanied by a claim to special cognitive status. They are not subject to ordinary, symmetrical rules of investigation. The phenomenon or the mediating individual, or the occasion, or the force itself, is claimed to be unique, and to possess a kind of sacredness or special quality which would be sullied by sceptical, unprejudicial inquiry. They claim to be sullied by a sceptical observer. Now of course we are in the presence of a kind of cognitive claim which, by the very manner in which it presents itself, excludes itself from the realm of reason. (The claim for special, impartial-inquiry-precluding status may of course be presented in rationalistic and hence seemingly scientific terminology, as a corollary of allegedly established facts, as happens in the case of psychoanalysis.) This does not mean of course that the phenomena invoked may not on occasion be such that, *if* only they were investigated properly, they would then be found to be amenable to rational handling and survive it.

In practice, adherents of irrational cults of this kind do not often neatly opt for one of the two alternatives. Instead, their position is systematically ambiguous, and this kind of obscurity and evasion and oscillation is part of its habitual self-presentation. They employ a sliding-scale methodology. When findings are favourable, ordinary inquiry is invited; when they are not, the special nature of the force – its shyness of sceptics – is invoked. A boat with well-trimmed sails will benefit from favourable winds, but escape the force of hostile squalls. The sails of unreason are often exceedingly well set.

The data and problems and theories which inspire many such groups are selected on a strange principle: they are chosen for their seeming violation, not so much of specific current scientific theories, but of the wider rational spirit itself, of the very expectation of order and intelligibility. The exceptional nature of particular data is then invoked to justify evasion of ordinary testing. Under modern conditions, many of these cults flourish, and often combine their pursuit of the exotic with the use of super-sophisticated anti-rationalist theories drawn from the formal high culture of the society.[1]

The triangular relations between rationalism, centralized authoritarian faith, and freelance magic and superstition, are complex and unstable. In any triangular political situation, alliances tend to be unstable and volatile: any two participants in the game may find it advantageous to gang up against the third. In the seventeenth century, contrary to the Weberian theory on which we have in the main been relying, the wilder forms of superstition were often aligned with the new rationalism.[2] Alliances will no doubt continue to oscillate.

---

[1] T. Luhrmann, *Persuasions of the Witch's Craft: Ritual magic and witchcraft in present-day England* (Blackwell, Oxford, 1989).

[2] R. Popkin, 'The third force in seventeenth-century thought: scepticism, science and millenarianism', in *The Prism of Science*, ed. E. Ullman-Margalit, Boston Studies in the Philosophy of Science, vol. 95 (D. Reidel, Boston, 1986).

3   Reason against Experience

The wider public is conscious primarily of the conflict between Reason and Authority. What seems to matter most is the choice between the final appeal to each free autonomous mind, and the final appeal to the Exceptional and Sacred Source. This conflict became acute in the seventeenth century, raged in the eighteenth, and pervaded politics in the nineteenth. By and large, adherents of the established order were also supporters of Authority in matters of belief, and social reformers were liberals in the theory of knowledge. The conflict has become muted or attenuated in our century, when many religions (with the notable exception of Islam) have markedly reduced the nature of their claims, when political authoritarianism has often invoked mundane rather than Revealed authority, and when social radicals have on occasion spurned rationality of belief. Nevertheless, this is still the form in which the wider public perceives the problem of Reason.

But within philosophy, the most debated issue is that between Reason and *Experience*. Both appeal equally to 'Reason' in the previous sense: to a publicly, symmetrically accessible court of appeal or decision procedure. They share the assumption that the final judgement lies with the ordinary mind, rather than some Special Fount of Truth. But the question is – what methods does or should this mind employ? Should it above all *think* clearly, using disputably lucid and unquestionable conceptual links as a kind of cognitive handrail, as Descartes taught, or should it fall back on 'experience', which was the doctrine of the great British empiricists?

Descartes and Hume are of course characteristically opposed to each other on this question. Descartes commended cogent reasoning above all, whilst Hume is presented as the arch-empiricist, who would subject all problems to the single test of experience. Experience is, for empiricists, precisely that which replaces authority; it constitutes a new and perfectly legitimate authority. Authority is dead, long live Authority! The notion of a unique cognitive Sovereign is retained. Only his identity changes.

The conflict over reason and experience plays itself out both in psychology and in the theory of knowledge, and in ways that are far from identical, though they are frequently confused or conflated. In psychology, one asks only how the mind actually works. One can then propose either an empiricist or a rationalist model. In the former case, one sees its working in terms of accumulation of data (empiricism); in the latter, in terms of a pre-wired, pre-programmed structure (rationalism). For instance, Noam Chomsky's theory of language is rationalist in this sense, and it is for this reason that he likes to invoke Descartes as an ancestor.[1] His basic evidence for such a view is that the astonishing range of competence of the human mind simply cannot be accounted for by the empiricist or 'accumulative' model: the assumption of 'pre-wiring' is, he convincingly argues, inescapable.

But even if this is true, which I think it is, it does not make rationalism true as an account of the *validation* of cognitive claims: the grammatical pre-wiring of a mind in no way prejudges the truth of assertions to which it gives its assent. It may predetermine the limit of affirmations which a mind can articulate, or it may even determine which ones it chooses; but that is another matter. I may well be 'pre-wired' to give my assent to a certain idea. This in no way renders that idea valid, though it may make its endorsement inescapable for me.

The confusion of the two issues, though indefensible, is widespread. For instance, many behaviourists in psychology believed that in order to vindicate free, empirical, fact-respecting inquiry into the human mind, they must also uphold the view that all human responses must be reactions to prior stimuli, and be explicable in no other way. Otherwise, there would be ideas in the mind which were not previously in the senses. It is assumed somehow that their self-generated presence in the mind would validate them, and so knowledge would bypass experience. To prevent such a possibility, which they abhorred, only ideas previously present in the senses may be permitted to exist! Paradoxically, the empiricist doctrine of the sovereignty of testing is here allowed to generate, *a priori*, a theory concerning the

---

[1] N. Chomsky, *Cartesian Linguistics* (Harper and Row, New York and London, 1966).

content of our minds and the mechanism of our mental processes!
In other words, the idea of any 'pre-wiring' must be repudiated
so as to protect the cognitive sovereignty of experience. In fact,
it is exceedingly improbable that a stimulus-response psychology
could possibly do justice to human conduct: but this in no way
undermines the view that all theories must in the end be checked
against facts. The source of our ideas is one issue; their validity,
quite another. An extreme version of the pre-wiring theory might
make truth inaccessible to us, or might entail that we could only
stumble on truth by accident, without any way of really knowing
whether we have really stumbled on it: but it would not prejudge
the nature of truth. The real situation seems to be that we are
pre-wired, *and* yet capable of attaining truth. How this is possible
constitutes an interesting problem which I cannot solve here (not
for lack of space, but of ability).

So we must first of all separate the psychological issue concerning how the mind actually works (is it pre-wired?), from the quite
distinct philosophical issue concerning what in the end validates cognitive claims (is it facts, or is it cogency of reasoning?).
It now seems overwhelmingly plausible that the mind is indeed
pre-wired, but this in now way on its own undermines the plausibility of the empiricist claim that only facts are, in the end, legitimate arbiters in disputes concerning what the world is like.

However, what really concerns us here is the clear separation of
the Reason-Authority confrontation from the Reason-Experience
dispute. They are largely independent of each other. The claims
that *either* experience *or* reasoning constitutes the final court of
appeal for our cognitive claims are equally in conflict with the
attribution of terminal authority to some sacred person, tradition,
institution, event, or other channel of revelation. A society which
recognizes and enforces a Fount of Authority, whether it be a
Person, a Text, an Event, or an Institution (or some combination
of these), is profoundly different from one which recognizes only
some faculty, whatever it be, located in principle in all men. Likewise, the denial of the authority of revelation does not on its own
tell us whether the final court of appeal is to be the lucidity and
cogency of ideas, or the availability of factual evidence.

A further grave complication in this matter is the ambiguity of the term 'experience'. In daily life, it is the name for convictions and attitudes acquired under the impact of the vicissitudes of life. Karl Popper's favourite quotation from Oscar Wilde – 'experience is the name people give to their mistakes' – is an echo of this. Popper of course values this saying precisely because he inverts its sense. Wilde's joke hinges on the fact that only *hurtful* events are classed as 'experience'. Other events simply illustrate how things are, and do not come to be classed as 'experiences'. Popper's point is that events *as such* constitute negative refutations or tests for science. This is their role in the growth of knowledge. Science cannot really tell us with finality and generality how things are. It can only find out how things are *not*. Theories are eliminated, but never definitively established. Experience can tell us of our mistakes, but not, with finality, of our successes.

The empiricist philosophers, following the Cartesian trail of purifying our convictions from corruption, replaced experience in the Oscar Wilde sense – unfortunate, upsetting disappointments – by the notion of a refined, 'pure' experience, within which data are purged of the contingent interpretative accretions. Nature speaks to us through them, unsullied by custom.

A very great deal depends on whether or to what extent such a purification is indeed possible. If it is, empiricism possesses a plausible solution to the problem of rationalism: it has discovered a compelling, impersonal, publicly available, symmetrical arbiter of cognitive claims. Purified experience is to perform this task. It is to be the court of appeal which will, in a fair, impartial, and convincing manner, settle disputes between men concerning the true nature of things. If on the other hand the purification is not feasible, if 'experience' speaks but with the voice of the prejudices with which it has become impregnated, it can hardly claim to arbitrate between sets of cultural prejudice. Corrupt judges are useless. Once again, that which would free us from doubt turns out, on examination, to be but another Voice of the Deceiver.

4   Reason against Emotion

This issue concerns the conduct of life, more than the discovery of truths. But the problems are connected. Emotion, intuition, flair, feeling, are sometimes credited, notably but not exclusively by romantics, with an important role in the discovery and formulation, or even in the assessment, of cognitive claims. *Gefuehl ist Alles*. In the main, however, the *homme moyen sensuel* of our society believes, roughly, that reason is appropriate in finance, but less so in the choice of marriage partner. It is, however, widely acknowledged that some men choose investments by intuitive hunches, and partners by cold calculation. There are good reasons why a society with a genuinely free marriage and sexual market should make a cult of the *coup de foudre*: it provides us with an excuse for *not* propositioning otherwise suitable partners, without giving undue offence. Men do not only rationalize their feelings: they also emotionalize their reasons.

The classical rationalists preferred the cool, 'rational' state of mind, which in their view favoured cognitive endeavour, and did not hamper thought by over-exciting it; such a state of mind also had a good deal to be said for it in morals. Descartes's identification of the self with the thinking substance encouraged our identification with our intellectual faculties, rather than with our darker passions. His follower Spinoza went far in devising a rational strategy for the conduct of life. He took over Descartes's idea of rational thought and of its powers, and simplified his metaphysics, elegantly reducing the number of substances from two to one: but he then adapted it all to a process of self-analysis, intended to lead to self-understanding, mastery, and rational contentment or acceptance. In effect he adapted Descartes's tools to the old ideal of philosophy as the recipe for the rational Good Life and self-sufficiency, and provided a new Handbook on How to be a Sage. The Sage found fulfilment through Reason.

It is at this point, the use of reason for the choice as well as the attainment of the Good Life, that Hume and Kant diverge fundamentally. Hume's deployment of reason told him firmly that all human *preferences* were independent, self-sufficient 'existences'. Reason could never determine, from its own powers, whether or not such putative existences really did exist. Our preferences were independent matters of fact, and they *existed*, if they did exist at all, in the form of feelings within us. Hence, only observation could tell us which ones actually existed and impelled us: no amount of *thought* could do so. So we could only *observe*, and never *think*, our way to the recognition of our aims and values. Hume supposed that rationalist ethics were a confusion, arising from faulty introspection: some inner 'passions', felt preferences, were so calm and tranquil, that they appear to our inner eye to resemble rational inference, and are mistakenly assimilated to it.

But reason could not really tell us either what we should do or what we should prefer. This was a *matter of fact*, and the relevant facts were located within us. The only available empirical basis for a preference was our *feeling*. Hence our feelings, or some sub-set of them, constituted the only possible basis of morality. This was one of the main points of origin of the important Utilitarian tradition in moral philosophy. Starting from the point that man is a sentient being, it concluded that what ultimately, or even exclusively, concerns man is the satisfactory state of his sensations and feelings. Ratiocination cannot possibly endow him with any aims or satisfactions: it only helps him select his means.

Kant took a different view. Sensations and feelings could not possibly provide the foundation for morals. We could not identify with our feelings: these are contingent, accidental, and outside our control. You might as well identify with your National Insurance (or Social Security) number. Kant required a self somewhat more substantial, more reliable, more weighty, than the mere Humeian 'bundle' of perceptions. A Customs Union is not a homeland, and a bundle is not a self. Kant was rather Cartesian in his tastes, and shared the aversion to granting authority to Custom and Example: our soul could not be located in the accidental and the contingent. It is outside history; we are visitors to rather than members of nature. Feelings, being contingent, variable, accidental, and diverse, could never be the basis of a demanding morality of absolute obligation. The puritanism of his ethics was a corollary of his fastidiousness concerning identity. Kant preferred to define morality in terms of the compulsion to treat like cases alike, a capacity which distinguishes a rational being from a merely sentient one. The capacity to impose *rules* on material makes us decent, and it also enables us to attain a level of comprehension which is a worthy foundation of our human identity. The crucial fact for Hume and the Utilitarians was that man was a *sentient* being; for Kant, that he was *rational*.

Whatever technical difficulties Kant's philosophy might encounter at this point, there can be no doubt that sociologically it was a more accurate expression of the spirit of the age than the *apparent* sensualism of the empiricists. Even Hume, technically an emotionalist/sensualist, who could not formally admit anything other than feeling to be the basis of either conduct or morality, in practice smuggled something like the Kantian requirement of symmetry into his moral philosophy. Not any old feelings, but the impartial feelings of the *disinterested observer*, were to be the basis of morality.

The issue which separates Hume and Kant at this point was due to acquire great importance later, and retains it to this day. What we face here is the problem of our identity. What part of ourselves is it exactly with which we can genuinely identify? In Descartes, the main problem concerned knowledge: the questions about Reason related to its status as a reliable and exclusive source of truth. Moral problems, though not absent, were not quite so central. In Kant, as in his sociological follower Durkheim, the problem of the legitimacy of knowledge and of a valid, binding identity become intimately linked.

So the issue which now emerged concerned reason, not only as a source of information, but also as a source of *identity*. With which part of ourselves can we really identify ourselves? Reason had deprived us of our erstwhile manifest identity by cutting us off from the constant and repeatedly reinforced endorsement of our role by 'custom and example', by culture; it was hoped that it would also provide us with a new one. Identity in the past had been confirmed and mirrored by the social and natural world; man knew the world, and knew it securely, and in turn, the world illuminated his place within itself, and thereby firmly conferred an identity on him. The socially imposed vision of the order of things, both natural and social, also ascribed and enforced human roles, so that a man's identity, his place in the general scheme, came as an indivisible whole which he could hardly refuse. But a cognitively fluid and unstable world, and a cold and impersonal one to boot, no longer provided this service. In a world over which socially underwritten and enforced Authority presided, identity was conferred and ascribed. It came in a package with the entire structure and generation of both nature and society: we had our place in the system, and this told us just who we were. Now, a world suspended by sustained, open-ended, interminable inquiry, a world made uncertain and unpredictable, and in a society no longer endowed with stable and sanctioned statuses, there was nothing any longer to confer a role and self-image on each man. The old world had ranked and numbered seats; the new one only provided a free-for-all chaos. The old world was like a dinner with *placement*, which tells you pretty unambiguously who you are, whilst the present one allows and imposes an undignified or unstable scramble for places and identities. Identity crises were not encouraged in the past, not really tolerated. Now they are *de rigueur*. So is the self a bundle, as Hume taught, or is it the invisible inner agency which both assembles the world and dictates our values, as Kant claimed? Hume and Kant responded to the same problem, but with diverging answers.

In this form and others, the Reason-Emotion confrontation was due to remain with us. It assumes a new form when the post-Darwinian inclusion of man in nature both devalued our 'higher' faculties and conferred a kind of new respectability on the 'lower' ones. At any rate, there was no longer any good reason to look down on them. Their erstwhile betters had been demoted to the same level. Where does the self truly reside? The debate was eventually pursued in an idiom indebted more to Nietzsche and Freud than to Hume and Kant.

5   Reason against piecemeal trial-and-error procedures

What we have here is, in effect, the opposition of system and method to unsystematic experimentation. This also is an issue which is much present in popular consciousness, and one which springs to people's minds when rationality is mentioned. The rational is the methodical, as opposed to reliance on hunches and a relapse into disorder.

This links up with the Reason/Emotion confrontation, in as far as hunches are based on feelings; it also overlaps with the opposition between centralized order and the voice of tradition, which gives priority to precedent, however untidy, over deliberate plan and system. Nevertheless, it is not identical with either. One important aspect of American Pragmatism, for instance, is the cult of the piecemeal approach, and the abjuring of the allegedly harmful old habit of seeking the support of general, sustaining, all-embracing principles. But Pragmatism certainly is not traditionalist. It commends opportunism with an American face.

Reason observed

A certain image of Reason is now emerging. One may adapt the question, allegedly asked by de Maistre about Nature, to Reason – *qui est donc cette dame?* We are now in a position to offer, albeit hesitantly and provisionally, a sketch portrait of the lady.

There is something inherently *generic* about her rational procedures. There would be something odd in classifying a single success, attained without the use of any general considerations, as 'rational'. The lady is also demanding: though she can be defied, and some do defy her habitually, it cannot be done lightly or without some loss. She is insistent and demanding, though her claim to dominion over us is also much challenged by other forces. Her demands are painful, and obedience is seldom rewarded. According to Hume, she is silent about values. Her procedures are also somehow self-justifying; they must not be arbitrary. As the regress of justification must end somewhere, a rational procedure should somehow carry its own justification in itself, as Descartes thought it could. She is also, like justice, symmetrical in her dealings; she does not stoop to partiality. She is tidy and systematic: what she does, fits into a wider order.

And the final, and perhaps most important trait: there is something *transcendent* about what she does. Her authority is not restricted to the bounds of her host body or her milieu. The criteria she deploys, the truths she attained, are not tied to the organism, social or other, within which she happens to be functioning. The validity of her operations is not tied to the whims or even permanent requirements of the host organism, whether it be biological or social. Yet she also has a preference for individualism and equality: her symmetrical availability to all, her even-handedness, her independence, preclude any cognitive personal hierarchy.

4
The Mundane Enemies of Reason

The spirit of history

The version of Reason, as so far impressionistically described, is the one available in the respectable mainstream tradition of rationalism. The path which leads from Descartes through Kant to Weber shows us reason as something clear, orderly, and individualist: a kind of lucid, self-guaranteeing agency, transparently at work in self-sufficient and autonomous minds, operating on their own.

But not all those who invoke her name are quite so fastidious: there are also other intellectual traditions, which constitute what might be called the wilder shores of Reason. They present a Reason more gregarious, less fastidious in its choice of means and less lucid in expression, and rather more involved in the hurly-burly of history.

The main example of this somewhat deviant, but historically important, tendency is to be found in the philosophy of Hegel, and in that of some of his successors and intellectual descendants. Here we encounter a Reason which is no longer individualist. In order to understand what Hegel and Hegelianism are about, one must, once again, begin with Kant.

Kant's central message was that the human self is to be identified with reason and rationality. Our sensual inclinations and perceptions were a bit of an incubus, indispensable, something we receive from outside, not perhaps necessarily with distaste, but certainly without being able to identify with it fully. To use the terms of a later thinker, they are *id*, and not *ego*. Our morality consists of rational orderliness, of not allowing any exceptions or asymmetry in the formulation of our choice of our aims and policies. Our moral style is to resemble our cognitive strategy, which calls for symmetrical, even-handed treatment and an orderly system. Such conduct is binding on us because, in implementing it, we express ourselves as we truly are. In this way, and this way alone, do we manifest our genuine identity. This true identity of ours is located in our capacity to impose symmetrical order on things. We *are* the imposition of order on the brute raw material of humanity. Order is Reason, and Reason is *ourselves*: disorder is the other, the Alien, whose intrusion diminishes us.

What is very awkward and problematic for this Kantian vision is the relationship between this identity-bearing and identification-worthy rational self on the one hand, and the natural, sensuous self on the other. The former is the bearer and the subject of rational and moral compulsion. The latter is a-moral and, as it were, mechanical. The problem of how the thinking and the material substance could possibly interact was already acute for Descartes; and in this new version, it was also due to become such for Kant. Neither could really solve it.

This problem of the mutual accommodation of the rational and the natural is Hegel's starting point. A large part of his appeal lay in his claim to have overcome it. For Kant, the two realms and, in effect, the two selves, coexisted in a most awkward way. We were doomed to an eternal bifurcation, an uneasy and awkward coexistence, unsweetened by *détente*. For Hegel, their relationship became both more interesting and less stable. It changes over time, and it is this transformation, the perpetual growth of rationality over historic time, which constitutes the secret of history. An impersonal Reason pervades the social world, and it does so to an ever-growing extent as time goes on: and it is this alone which confers meaning on history.

Hegel's second and related starting point is the emerging idea of Progress, the supposition, gradually imposing itself on the European mind at the turn of the eighteenth and nineteenth centuries, that history is the story of sustained and continuous improvement, of which they, the modern Europeans, were both heroes and beneficiaries. This idea is one of the most magnificent, most attractive theodicies, or justifications of the ways of God or of the world to man, ever invented. It endows the conflicts, sufferings and tribulations of mankind with justification, by turning these evils into the spurs and the obstacles, and the means of the great and gradual fulfilment of mankind, sustained in its upward historical struggle. Without such spurs and challenges, there could have been no strife and striving, and hence also no fulfilling achievement. Hegel vigorously committed himself to this view:

> We must bring to history the belief and conviction that the realm of the will is not at the mercy of contingency. That world history is governed by an ultimate design, that it is a rational process – whose rationality is not that of a particular subject, but a divine and absolute reason – that is a proposition whose truth we must assume; its proof lies in the study of world history itself, which is the image and enactment of reason.[1]

When opting for the idea that history is the fulfilment of an ultimately beneficial plan, it is noteworthy that Hegel chose the language of *Reason*. The plan implemented in history is not that of any one concrete person, but of an impersonal spirit, which, it would seem, is Reason. Reason has replaced the deity as the Great Schemer who guides history. It *is* the deity, and deity lives on through it.

In this way, the idea of the fulfilment of historic plan is brought in to solve the Kantian problem of how the rational and the natural could ever meet. They meet in history: the ever-

---

[1] G.W.F. Hegel, *Lectures on the Philosophy of World History* (Cambridge University Press, Cambridge, 1975; first published 1837).

increasing permeation of the world by Reason constitutes the explanation of that progress which seemed to become increasingly manifest in the development of Europe. Instead of being separate, parallel, incompatible and incommensurate, reason and nature, their interaction remaining an ever impenetrable mystery, as it was for Kant, now fuse and blend throughout history, and ever more so as time goes on. *This* is the true meaning of Progress. The sense of history is precisely this ever-increasing, and in the end complete, permeation of concrete history by the spirit of Reason. In this way, instead of living separate and distinct lives, doomed to an eternal apartheid, a fate to which, in their different ways, both Hume and Kant had consigned them, brute fact and reason could be seen as giving a most agreeable sense to history by their gradual, intermittently traumatic, but ever-growing and satisfying fusion.

A pretty picture. Such a hypothesis would seem at most times to be pure fantasy and wish-fulfilment. But it acquired an intoxicating element of plausibility to the European generations pondering the French and Industrial Revolutions. It had suddenly become plain that historic change is fundamental, irreversible and cumulative, and that it seemed to bestow upon mankind a new order, with a promise of a deeper and even more diffused human fulfilment. The notorious Hegelian doctrine that 'the Real is the Rational' is an expression of this view. So is the aphorism that initially only one was free, then some were free, and eventually, in the modern state, all were free. A person who took Cartesian and Kantian dualism seriously (as indeed it deserves), and was troubled by its problems, and who at the same time was swayed by the idea of historic Progress, must find Hegel appealing, notwithstanding the dogmatism of his claims, the obscurity of his affirmations, and the portentousness of his style. Perhaps, given the grandeur of the news he was bringing, a suitably elevated and intimidating style, incomprehensible yet suggestive, the verbal equivalent of trumpets, was altogether appropriate.

The third element, which added both content and plausibility to the Hegelian doctrine, was the idea which sociologists later came to call latent function or functionality: the supposition that men, in their often quite self-centred and narrowly conceived actions, none the less unwittingly serve 'higher', that is more general and fundamental and long-term historical ends. In the old religious form, the idea was already perfectly familiar. The Europeans of the relevant generation saw what seemed to them a remarkable historical story of development, and they knew that very few men had consciously aimed at serving any such overall plan. Could not a mechanism inherent in history have used the more private, immediate, lowly ends of men, and tricked them into the service of a Higher Plan? Hegel called this the 'Cunning of Reason'. Adam Smith's idea of the Hidden Hand has a similar logic.

A fourth element which rather overlaps with all this is the notion of Culture: the idea of an impersonal, pervasive style of thinking, feeling, and acting, which permeates the minds of men without their being aware of it, and guides them in thought, feelings, and conduct. Descartes knew that an accumulated body of ideas and assumptions, later to be called 'culture', leads men to their convictions and comportment, and he spurned it as the prime fount of error. Hegel added the view that these accumulations formed systems, had their expression in social and political forms, and generated each other in a Grand Succession which endowed history and human life with its meaning. *Custom and example* continued and carried a deep wisdom, notwithstanding the superficial semblance of contingency and chaos. All this gave a kind of realistic, sociological content to the otherwise mystical idea of an impersonal spirit or Reason guiding the often blind, irrational and narrow conduct of men.

The generation to which Hegel belonged was one which had become very receptive to such a notion. It had trouble with the old deity, but was eager to find something it could worship. So the Spirit of an Age, its *culture*, was identified with the agency which was cunningly channelling the efforts of men in the service of a greater cause, the ever-increasing convergence of Reason and fact. Culture, which pervades men's thought, feeling and conduct, could in this way also at the same time be the puppet master of History. In suitably and decently obscure and edifying language, the Spirit of the Age was equated with the Guiding Agency of History, and both of them with the deity. it was quite useful *not* to know at all clearly just which of these one was actually addressing in prayer. The precise object of worship could vary with the sophistication, or even the mood, of the believer.

The old deity, simultaneously personified and hidden, was taken to be a code term for a guiding impersonal culture-spirit which guides and bestows meaning on history. Peasants, who would not have understood Hegel even if his thoughts were patiently explained to them, had to personify this impersonal Reason; better talk to them of the God of Abraham than of culture and latent function, as the explanatory notions of history. They really wouldn't follow all that stuff. At the same time, the learned did not need to disavow the personal God of their fathers, knowing that He was really just a code term for the latest philosophical discovery. So all was well, many times over.

Thus the doctrine contained a way of obfuscating the confrontation of religion and science/scholarship, of the problem of the loss of faith, *and* at the same time a means of remedying the Disenchantment of the World, implicit in the separation of Reason and Nature. The impersonal Agency was the Spirit of the Age, or rather, it successively manifested itself in a whole *series* of such Spirits. It was really only a spirit with a succession of incarnations. Each of them was but its temporary avatar. But it could also be identified with the Author and Producer of the great historical drama itself, *and* it could constitute its ultimate culmination. It gave all of us whatever meaning our life might ever claim, by assigning us our place and role in history, and making history into a revelation of a plan both divine and yet endogenous, self-generating, self-completing. The world was One, yet not bereft of God.

This view enabled men to maintain their previous religious affiliation and identity by treating the old theological convictions as parables for the newly revealed Hegelian truth. The God of the Old Testament had revealed Himself only in a restricted part of the world and history. The Hegelian Absolute Spirit which pervaded an enriched and broadened history, above all the European sequel, was somewhat ambiguously identified with the more concrete God of Abraham. So those wishing to remain loyal to Him would at the same time share in the latest philosophic fashion: the God of the philosophers and the God of Abraham had, at long last, become one and the same.

This, in substance, was the Hegelian doctrine. Of its historical significance there can be no doubt at all. It provided much of the idiom for the politically potent ideology of nineteenth-century nationalism. Modified and 'stood on its head' by Marx, whose intellectual generation had been bewitched by this vision, it engendered the most important political philosophy of the new age, and became for a time a major new world religion, and, for a time, the official faith of a large number of important societies.

The somewhat ambiguous nature of that famous Marxist 'standing on its head' of Hegel also enabled the two founding fathers of Marxism to 'establish' historical materialism. The curious fact is that the ideas contained within that phrase are supported by mere affirmation, and not by evidence. The reason why it was possible to persuade so many people by mere affirmation is this: there are at least two, and not one, distinctions contained in the opposition of materialism and idealism. One issue leads to the question, Is the driving motor of history some impersonal 'spirit', as the Hegelians had claimed in their metaphysical intoxication, or is it the concrete needs and activities of men?

People under the influence of Hegel could easily understand this question, and many were no doubt ready to answer, Yes, of course, *obviously* it is the latter. Such is in substance the message of Marx and Engels's *The German Ideology*:

> In direct contrast to German philosophy which descends from heaven to earth, here we ascend from earth to heaven...We set out from real, active men, and on the basis of their real life-process we demonstrate the development of the ideological reflexes and echoes...Morality, religion, metaphysics, all the rest of ideology... no longer retain the semblance of independence.[1]

---

[1] K. Marx and F. Engels, *The German Ideology* (Lawrence and Wishart, London, 1938, 1942, repr. 1965; written 1845–6).

The rival theory had been but a mystification. Its denial seems endowed with a self-evident quality. Whether true or not, the 'materialist' position, in *this* rather special sense, at least seems endowed with an overwhelming and seemingly irresistible persuasiveness. Marx and Engels in *The German Ideology* certainly presented the matter in this light. Real men, not abstractions, make history.

But there is another and quite independent issue: are economic factors dominant in history, or are there others – for instance, the means of coercion – which are equally important, or perhaps more important? This question has no immediately obvious answer. On the contrary, the issue is very difficult, and could only be answered, if at all, with the help of a great deal of historical evidence and very careful analysis. Coercion is as real and concrete an activity as production.

But by a curious sleight of hand, the founding fathers of Marxism succeeding in prejudging it. They extended the plausibility of the 'materialist' answer in the first and rather less contentious sense, concerning the role of abstractions in history, to this other and far more problematic issue. The denial of our domination by *abstractions* (plausible, though not wholly uncontentious either) was extended by this verbal sleight of hand to the denial of the autonomous role of *coercion* in history. Because production trumps abstraction (plausible), it also trumps violence (most contentious). By obscuring the deep differences between the two issues, they committed themselves to the following inference: *because* history is made by concrete men and not by abstract spirits, *therefore* production dominates coercion. It does not follow in the very least, but much of the erstwhile appeal of Marxism hinges on this confusion. It is most appealing to the spirit of a bourgeois age: the middle classes live by work, not by robbery, and are pleased to learn that productive work, not violence, *really* governs history. It is the bourgeois value of *production*, not the feudal-aristocratic value of violent *coercion*, which is the ultimate secret and master of history!

It is this *léger-de-main* which gives us the Marxist promise of salvation for mankind. Force and violence cannot, *cannot* operate independently in history. It is only a symptom, a side-effect, of the mal-functioning of the productive process. That mal-functioning in turn is said to be providentially self-correcting, or at least will be such in the very end. Therefore salvation, a coercion-free and exploitation-free social order, in which the real human potentialities for full self-expression can flourish without let or hindrance, is our guaranteed, though alas much-delayed birthright, which in the fullness of time will be bestowed upon us. The Marxists borrowed their provisional pessimism about contemporary bourgeois society from certain themes in classical economics,[1] but their ultimate optimism from Hegel.

In the Marxist version of the Hegelian doctrine of a historic plan, the whole mystical notion of a pervasive and dominant Spirit is of course no longer conspicuously present. Nevertheless, a good deal of the Hegelian type of rationalism survives. The idea that history is not an accidental accumulation of events, but the fulfilment of an immanent plan, which uses participants as agents of its own without their knowledge or consent, is retained. This great plan confers meaning and justification on human striving, and conduces to a satisfactory final condition.

Should this kind of doctrine, of which the Hegelo-Marxist tradition is the most prominent example, be considered a form of 'rationalism', and receive prolonged treatment in a study of rationalism? This is largely a matter of definition.[2] Some of the features we have provisionally allocated to 'Reason' are conspicuously absent from this doctrine. It is often mystical in content, and frequently arbitrary and obscure in its assertions. It neither preaches nor practises rationality, even if it usurps its name. It lacks individualism, it lacks clarity, let alone the luminous, self-sustaining and persuasive clarity which was demanded by Descartes. It lacks that pursuit of cultural transcendence, of

---

[1] cf. E.A. Wrigley, *People, Cities and Wealth: The transformation of traditional society* (Blackwell, Oxford, 1987).

[2] For a more favourable assessment of this tradition, see H. Marcuse, *Reason and Revolution: Hegel and the rise of social theory* (Oxford University Press, Oxford, 1941; repr. Routledge and Kegan Paul, London, 1955).

independent non-circular cogency, which is such an important trait of rationality. On the contrary, it solves the problem of knowledge by identifying truth with the dictates of a World Spirit alias Historic Process. It lacks any real transcendence in its own procedures, for it consists of a circle of self-sustaining ideas, devoid of any genuine external and independent confirmation. The essence of the Cartesian tradition was the supposition that a cognitive *procedure* existed which stood outside the world and any one culture, and was capable of independent judgement of cognitive claims about the world. This transcendent faculty alone was sovereign. The Hegelo-Marxist tradition by contrast absolutizes a process within the world (and thereby, affirmations about it), elevating it above mere procedural rules, cognitive or other. The elevation of substantive, 'class' truth and justice above more 'formalistic' procedural principles was indeed a marked, and most repulsive trait of Marxist societies. Practice did indeed become one with theory.

The arguments for excluding this tradition of thought from Rationalism proper are strong, and many would find them persuasive. I find them convincing enough, and I feel little attraction for this tradition. None the less, this peculiar and curious sense of Rationalism, inspired by the notion of an impersonal, collective, cunning Agency behind history, is endowed with sufficient historic links to the more legitimate forms of Rationalism, to warrant a critical inclusion in any survey of the forms of rationalism. One ought to know how it relates to rationalism proper, and how it emerged from it, and how it lays claim to the name of Reason. If one ignored it altogether, one might fail to understand much of the debate.

Dark gods against Reason

The Reason-Nature confrontation that took place in seventeenth- and eighteenth-century thought lies also at the starting point of another development – one that leads to what is perhaps the most influential form of modern irrationalism. Kantian dualism is rooted in the opposition of Reason and Nature: reason can know the world only in an orderly manner, as an orderly system. Thereby it engenders Nature – that is, a rule-bound orderly system of phenomena – as the only possible object of knowledge. The orderliness of the investigating mind, tidily arranging data under rules which are intended to form a system, are reflected in a world which is itself tidy and symmetrical, in which no facts escape a shared order.

But within such an orderly Nature, there is no room for either reason or morality, or indeed for a genuine identity. A big orderly machine has room only for further small machines within itself, never for persons. It has room for mechanisms which *obey* natural laws: it has no room at all for beings which autonomously *conceive* laws, natural and moral, and which freely and rationally choose to conform to the latter.

So Reason has to be declared extra-territorial by Kant: it thus becomes the only possible bearer of our identity, our responsibility, our cognitive competence and capacity for moral choice. It alone can *know* Nature: but by the same token, there is no room for it *within* Nature. Nature has no place for either knowledge or moral choice. This was Kant's problem.

The Kantian solution was a desperate one. He said that as objects in nature, we had to see ourselves as things amongst others, law-bound and mechanical. As inquirers and moral agents, we had to think of ourselves as standing outside nature. In a new form, Kant repeated the Cartesian 'cosmic exile'. For Kant, it is no longer an intellectual experiment, a cognitive self-purification: it is the permanent condition and predicament of each human being. We had to *assume* that we possessed an extra-territorial identity, for otherwise neither knowledge nor morality were conceivable; but, by the very terms of reference of the problem, we could never encounter and experience these bearers of our identity. (In knowledge and in moral endeavour, we saw its fruits, but we could *only* see its fruits, and never the thing itself.) I know of no better solution. Whether or not it is acceptable, it does highlight the most important point about Reason: it is self-devouring, because it engenders a world in which there is no room for itself.

One way to escape from the painful dualism was taken, as we saw, by Hegel: he proposed that, far from being destined for an eternal separation from the world, Reason *increasingly* permeates the world, and gradually reveals itself within it. But quite a different path was taken by Hegel's passionate rival and denouncer, Arthur Schopenhauer.[1] He abandoned Kant's tortuous attempts at finding a bridge between the self as reason and the self as part of nature. He gave up the effort to show how a rational being could miraculously both act morally, and be part of a merely causal, mechanical world. He refrained from trying to squeeze reason-inspired moral action into some interstice of a compact world of blindly, causally controlled fact. He forsook the Kantian enterprise of forcing a wedge of rationality into a tightly packed realm of brute fact. Gone is the tormented effort to make moral action appear possible, or rather, *thinkable*.

Morality itself, however, is not abandoned; but it is no longer envisaged as a special kind of action, transcending nature. Instead – a most elegant solution – it is redefined as *in*action, as passivity, as renunciation of the world, as the switch from action in the world, to mere *contemplation*. He might well have said: seekers of morality have tried to change the world, but henceforth they should merely try to contemplate it. So, in Schopenhauer, a modern theory of knowledge blends with the ancient pursuit of a personal and morally inspired escape from this Vale of Tears. The title of Schopenhauer's principal work, *The World as Will and Idea*,[2] conveys this alternative. There is no such thing as *good* willing: *all* willing is equally bad. Action is the expression of Will. Goodness of a kind does exist, however: but it is to be found, not in a special kind of willing, but in *abstention* from willing altogether. It is found in passive contemplation, in a turning from Will to Idea.

Schopenhauer introduced, or rather blended, a number of

---

[1] See for instance B. Magee, *Men of Ideas: Some creators of contemporary philosophy* (BBC Books, London, 1978); *The Philosophy of Schopenhauer* (Clarendon Press, Oxford, 1983).

[2] Arthur Schopenhauer, *The World as Will and Idea* (first published 1818).

themes. First, there is the Buddhist and Platonic high valuation of contemplation as contrasted with action, and there is the Indian idea of salvation through self-exile: he was the first major modern Western philosopher to be profoundly influenced by Eastern thought. The Hellenic-Indian high valuation of contemplation also blends with a characteristically nineteenth-century aestheticism, of salvation conceived on the analogy of admiring an *objet d'art*. Life is indeed a predicament rather than a spectacle, but salvation can be had (at most) in redressing the balance, and turning the predicament into a spectacle. As spectator, the collection-owner fuses with the sage.

Second, whereas Descartes had exiled himself for *cognitive* purposes, but morally speaking retained his French citizenship, it was Schopenhauer who turned to the idea that philosophical Inner Emigration was moral, even more than it was epistemic. There is in his thought a pessimism which abjures the idea of any improvement of the world, let alone a major and guaranteed Trend in such a direction, in other words the idea of Progress. One does not emigrate from a successful going concern; or if one does, one is loth to admit that it is successful. Schopenhauer emigrates from the world not so much in pursuit of knowledge but in flight from pain. The idea of Progress is totally absent from Schopenhauer's thought, and it is firmly repudiated. The world is left to the devil. There is no purpose in it, and there is certainly no salvation through progress. There is no salvation at all within the world, either for individuals or collectivities, though there is salvation in opting out of it, and turning to contemplation and to the abstention from desire, which Schopenhauer preached rather more than he practised it. The fact that he failed to mortify his Will earned him the approval of his critical disciple Nietzsche.

Third, the blind world of causal nature is endowed with a kind of biological and proto-Darwinian metaphysic: all the pushing and striving in it is subsumed under a single and rather anthropomorphic term, *Will*. Thus it is in a way personified, or at any rate treated as a single, brutal, ever-unsatisfied, unappeasable and irresistible force, manifest everywhere, but quite specially visible in animal lust and aggression. It knows only unsatisfied tormented lust, and the void and lassitude following gratification: there is never any positive satisfaction in between. Schopenhauer is the philosopher of dissatisfied sexuality: there is no pleasure to be had in this world. There is only the mathematical, extensionless boundary between as yet unsatisfied, hungry, unfulfilled, tormented craving, and weary, depressed, satiated exhaustion. He altogether seems to ignore temporally extended pleasures, such as lying in a hot bath. This rather selective sensitivity is one of the bases of his famous pessimism.

The mathematician Descartes had reduced Nature to sheer extension, a world fit to be the home of geometrical forms. The proto-sociological Hegel handed over the world to an abstract spirit, half scheming Mechanism of History, half Pervasive Culture. In an age soon to be preoccupied with biology, and already much taken with dark romanticism, Schopenhauer reduced Nature to a blind generic lust and aggression, named Will. In human beings, this demiurge for some strange reason often turns in upon itself, and thus, oddly enough, also provides the only force capable of thwarting itself. There is no other, countervailing *good* force in the world which could do it: if Will is ever to be thwarted, it can only come about because Will has turned in upon itself. Freud was to say much the same. Schopenhauer and his successor Nietzsche both saw all this very clearly, but the two of them *evaluated* it very differently. When the Will turns in upon itself and thwarts itself, and the individual in question turns to passivity and contemplation, Schopenhauer looks on with approval; Nietzsche saw such ascetic morality as simply the devious and shifting pursuit of satisfaction of blind lust by other means, and spurned it, preferring the more candid and open manifestation of Will.

These ideas were destined for a great future. The notion of the world dominated by a blind animal driving force called Will had great appeal in a century in which biology for a time replaced physics as the science endowed with the greatest philosophic suggestiveness. The biological vision suggests that deep inner conflict arises not between Lower and Higher Forces, as Kant supposed, but between low forces and *other* low forces, somewhat more devious and nasty because they camouflage themselves, and give themselves spurious airs of a Higher Morality. The old Platonic question-begging grading, which accepted the super-ego at its own valuation, had now lost its foundation. All that happens is that *some* low forces know how to adopt a cunning and deceitful disguise. In an age in which nature would be seen as one and undivided, and man as very much part of it, such a doctrine was bound to be attractive. It endowed but recently naturalized man with flesh and blood. It devalued the pretension of an absolute and anti-nature ascetic morality.

The single, orderly, unified nature which is the product of the rational spirit could not really accommodate the desperate Kantian dualism that separates the self which *knows* the world and is capable of moral judgement from the self which inhabits it and is observable, and endows him with a higher authority; nor was it likely for very long to console itself by means of the Hegelian fairy tale, which assures us that Reason is the *régisseur* responsible for the *mise en scène* of history, with a Happy End guaranteed, one in which the Lower and the Higher eventually blend in harmony. But the new story about blind Will turning in upon itself, and masquerading as something Higher, whilst in reality only pursuing its low ends by other means – now this had a tremendous suggestiveness and appeal. It rang true, and had great psychological depth.

The thinker who seized on this most effectively was Schopenhauer's admiring disciple and follower, Nietzsche. In due course he stood Schopenhauer on his head, much as Marx had stood Hegel on his. If Nature contains nothing other than Will, why declare it all bad (as Schopenhauer had done), rather than all *good*? In the name of *what* exactly had Schopenhauer denounced the Will? In the name of the pursuit of self-assertion by the very same Will, only when using other – and devious – means? If everything's much the same, what's the odds? If everything is morally on the same level, why use the minus sign rather than the plus sign? Why use any evaluative sign at all? In the name of what exactly could the Will be condemned? There is nothing left to warrant such a condemnation. No vantage point remains from which such a denunciation could be issued.

Nietzsche went on to say that the resentful, devious, and

deceitful form of the will, which had turned in upon itself, and which had been *forced* so to turn in on itself by the weakness of the organism in which it found itself, was somehow even nastier, less healthy, than the candid, forthright, brutal Will of a vigorous, victorious being. If the nasty, deceitful and resentful form was none the less successful in its stratagem, it is far from clear how Nietzsche could consistently damn it: success, by whatever means, should be self-justifying. If successful, as Nietzsche regretfully admitted it to be, why should it be excoriated? Why should devious cunning be inferior to open, vigorous violence, if it is more effective? What else is there? If the resentfully cunning weak ones outwit the stupid brutes, well good luck to them... Why should not foxes rather than lions inherit the earth? It is unclear not merely how Nietzsche can allow himself this particular value judgement, but how on his premisses he can allow himself *any*.

But some kind of quite extraneous aesthetic criterion appears to be injected by Nietzsche into the argument: he seems to smuggle an extraneous vantage point for judgement into a world in which, by rights, there ought to be no space for it. He smuggles in an unwarranted premiss, much as Schopenhauer had done. Perhaps he could try to defend this by saying that the twisted self-tormenting form of the Will was pathogenic: it engendered disease and ugliness, and a loss of excellence. Even in this form, this would seem to amount to logical cheating. In a norm-less nature, there would be no criterion other than success. Aesthetic fastidiousness possesses no better justification than the old morality. But such was his position.

Ideas of this kind in the end reached an enormously wide public through Sigmund Freud. They had this impact because Freud disseminated them in medical and scientific, rather than in literary and philosophical, terminology. He made them part of medicine, or rather, claimed to have done so, and linked them to a therapeutic technique which promised relief for the unhappy individual. Very significantly, he also endowed these ideas with a ritual and a church. In Freud's hands, the somewhat nebulous and metaphysical Will (Schopenhauer) or Will-to-Power

(Nietzsche) was endowed with what at least looked like a very specific and empirically defined form, and was linked to sexuality. At least the reader knew where he was, or thought he did. More important, the havoc which both the deviousness and the thwarting of our psychic force wrought in our psyche could now, or so he claimed, be corrected by a technique specially designed to outwit that deviousness. The technique was declared to be in the keeping of a severely demarcated guild/sect. The technique may or may not have been well adapted to outwit its cunning opponent, but its deployment was governed by rules so defined as to make its effectiveness self-confirming; moreover, it was marvellously well adapted to the requirement of the age. The condition of successfully availing oneself of this therapy was in effect the abstention from scrutinizing its credentials and querying its success. He who tried to do either thereby showed that he failed to fulfil the conditions of therapy, and so had only himself to blame if it did not succeed.[1]

Freud had none of the philosophic coherence of Kant, nor the depth of Nietzsche. He did not seem to perceive how very much these insights, if valid, undermined our commitment to, or identification with, rationalistic values. He continued to uphold these values, and even practise them, and contented himself with showing the technical difficulties of doing so. He understood and underscored the heavy psychic price which had to be paid for the attempt to restrain the dark forces within us, but, being willing to pay that price, failed to appreciate that he had destroyed the logical necessity of doing so.

But the general lesson was exceedingly well and widely disseminated by his work: our seeming rationality and morality is but a fraud. In truth, it is but the pursuit of the satisfaction of the very same dark blind forces by other means. The forces underlying morality and abstract ideals were identical with those very drives which putative Reason, and traditional morality, claim to damn, spurn, and oppose. They only differed from them in their

---

[1] For a fuller formulation of this argument, see E. Gellner, *The Psychoanalytic Movement: Or the cunning of unreason* (Paladin, London, 1985).

deviousness, their dishonesty, and their tendency to engender psychic disease. The deviousness and disingenuousness of the claims of morality and reason deprives them of any real authority. Our true identity lies elsewhere. As Durkheim in effect argued that, in the sphere of knowledge, the aspiration of Reason to transcend society was but a hidden pursuit of social ends, so in the sphere of morals Freud stressed that the imperatives of Reason were but the pursuit of instinctive drives by other means.

In Freud's variant of the message, we can only communicate with our true and hidden identity, and ascertain its real wishes, by means of a curious technique, in the keeping of his own monopolistic Guild. It is revealed by a strange inner negotiation, under authorized guidance from a Guild member. Our 'true self' is emphatically no longer identified with the rational imposition of abstract general rules on drives, as Kant had taught. The ego is mysteriously self-defined, distilled by a compromise between desire and reality, whose precise formula remains a trade secret. One suspects that in clinical practice it is adjusted by the practitioners in the light of their clients' requirements, means, and possibilities.

Though Freud himself (consistently or otherwise) was no kind of irrationalist, his ideas constitute one of the most powerful, probably the most powerful, irrationalistic currents in the contemporary world. Our identity is not to be sought in Reason and in careful, tidy thinking, and certainly not in participation in a Historic Plan, nor in aesthetic contemplation (though Freud's own collection was outstanding). It does not lie either in rigid self-control or in antinomian indulgence, but in some unspecified intermediate point, to be privately and individually negotiated. The indeterminacy, and hence the convenient manipulability, of this morally optional point, surely made a major contribution to the highly successful marketing of this recipe for salvation.

In any case, our real personal fulfilment does not and cannot lie in the kind of comportment recommended in Descartes's rules, or the Kantian apotheosis of consistency, and even less in any utilitarian pleasure–pain accountancy. If society obliges us to behave in such ways in some measure, as it does, the psychic price involved is heavy indeed. Moreover, no accommodation with our condition is to be had by means of merely intellectual self-analysis and acceptance, as had once been commended by the Cartesian moralist Spinoza. Only (at best) a submission to qualified guidance and a turbulent catharsis can achieve such an end. The turbulence of the process, and the absence of public criteria for its correct conduct and termination, mean that in the course of it the sufferer must abandon his own autonomy and surrender to guidance. The concept of the 'Unconscious' devalues both the individual's autonomy and all inner rational compulsion, *and* the authority of evidence. He can never tell whether his inner conviction is not the voice of the Deceiver, nor can he be sure, whilst unaided, whether the evidence of actual behaviour is not merely 'superficial' and a piece of clever deceit. Only the licensed Practitioner (at best) can tell him, and, *ex hypothesi*, there is no appeal against his verdict. Nothing could be less Cartesian in spirit than such self-surrender and leap of faith.

So there is indeed a way towards attaining the kind of discovery about oneself which can then lead to an at least relative inner peace: but the path to it lies only through a deliberately counter-rational procedure (free-association and emotional catharsis). These constitute a kind of irrationalistic but purely *semantic* Saturnalia, in which logical order is not merely no longer imposed, but is actually *proscribed*. In the therapeutic procedure, the sustained inversion of all the canons of Protestant-Cartesian rationality – orderliness, restraint – marks and highlights the special condition, just as heightened formality and/or sartorial abandon had done in the more collective rituals of earlier mysteries.

But, in an individualistic age devoid of local or kin communities, the ritual is solitary, carried out by a single participant led by a single Guide. The successful execution and completion of this procedure requires this self-abandon of the self to unreason. In all this, the technique resembles the *rites de passage* of secret societies, which bind the adept by the terror and illogicality of their ritual, by the invasion of customary taboos. So, in the course of it all, Descartes's recommendations for the comportment of our intellectual life are systematically inverted. Revolution may be the festival of the oppressed, and psychoanalysis is the festival of the repressed.

The procedure also restores, in a new, non-religious terminology, the appeal to cognitive Authority: the technique only works under the supervision of a member of the sacramentally insulated Caste of Initiates. The training/initiation confers a distinctive and salvation-conferring psychic condition on them: it is, in effect, a sacrament. Claims can be checked, not by open criteria and against publicly available data, but only by esoteric principles and against data as interpreted by more authoritative members of the Caste itself. So the Caste itself sits in judgement on its own pronouncements, and it simply cannot, on its own terms, be challenged. As all this follows from the doctrine itself, it is impossible for the doctrine to be overturned. Self-confirmation can hardly go further.

Because of the marked lack of a centralized, authoritative, and hope-supplying vision of the world in our society (a lack which is inherent in its basic principles, and is not accidental), little or no well-organized provision of succour for the psychically distressed is available. At the same time, in consequence of obvious and familiar features of this society – mobility, instability, insecurity, competitiveness, absence of pervasive and sustaining local communities – those acutely distressed form a large, and no doubt constantly growing, proportion of the population. This creates an important market for solace, support, consolation, 'therapy'. This powerful and growing demand has inevitably called forth a supply.

The style, techniques, and idiom of a rapidly growing new secular pastoral profession, the 'counsellors', derives in very large part from the irrationalist tradition we have discussed, and which communicates with irrational hidden forces by means of untestable techniques. Pastoral services now claim to work by mediating with a hidden true self, not rational nor rationally manipulable, nor directly accessible by the unaided individual: and this self, though not fully identified with biological drives, is at least closer to them than it is to any formal rationality. How such a true self is distilled from those biologically given drives, and related to objective constraints and limitations, remains something of a mystery. In the main the new pastors are given, like Freud, to an uneasy retention of rationalist values, combined with a commitment to a picture of the human psyche which would seem to render those values irrelevant.

Therapeutic irrationalism

This topic really falls into two quite distinct parts. There is the content of Freudian doctrine, what it actually, substantively teaches; and there is its actual method and mode of operation. Though there are of course connections between the two, it is none the less important to separate them.

The substantive doctrine profoundly modifies the previously dominant image of man, which had indeed been much influenced by various currents of rationalism. This vision had presented man as a careful maximizer of pleasure and avoider of pain, or alternatively, in a more high-minded style, as a being which could find satisfaction in the implementation of noble and abstract ideals. The Freudian revelation warmly invites us to dismiss all of this as so much eyewash. The real springs of our motivation and satisfaction are linked on the one hand to instinctual needs and on the other to the concrete and intense relations and feelings, seldom avowed, which prevail in intimate groups. These, however, are perceived only in a distorting prism, as through a glass darkly: our lusts and relationships themselves ignore all proportion, perspective, and propriety, and moreover are seen only through a cunning self-imposed code, whose central purpose is to deceive. But it is these lusts and relations which really matter to us, and which are relevant to our mental balance or our loss of it, and which need to be considered when we cope with emotionally induced disease; the rest is but façade, deployed for deception and, above all, for self-deception.

Moreover, if we are in deep trouble, it is useless to comport ourselves in the manner commended by the rationalists. A cold, rational analysis of our aims and circumstances will never lead us to the real source of the disturbance, nor help us overcome it. It is never manifest nor accessible to direct approach. The effective corrective measures are not rational ones.

So much for the heart of the substantive doctrine. If valid, it undermines or destroys the major political ideologies both of the left and of the liberal right. Neither participation in a free and egalitarian community, nor acquisition of wealth or of gratifications, really appeases or gratifies the psyche. Ironically – given its hostility to Freud – it is the recipes of the new romantic, illiberal Right, the restoration of hierarchical, inegalitarian, ritualistic, emotive and violent politics, which really meets the true human requirements as revealed by the new vision of man. Mainly for racialist reasons, this kind of Right does not invoke Freud; in as far as it troubles to appeal to philosophical authority at all, it is liable to invoke the name of Nietzsche.

The Western liberal intelligentsia, which does recognize Freud, and which has adopted his language and ideas as the standard idiom for the handling of the human psyche and personal relations, has not embraced such political conclusions under his influence. On the contrary, the adoption of Freudian ideas is combined with, and even somehow used to justify, an extremely permissive moral liberalism. Roughly speaking, the modal use of Freud can be expressed by the formula 'Freud has shown repressions to be bad, therefore restrictions on conduct should be removed.' Though there is no warrant for this in the Master's doctrine or words, this is how, in effect, he has been interpreted and applied.

This leaves the issue of the irrationalism of Freudian method. The actually operative Freudian theory of knowledge contains both a partial adoption and partial inversion of Cartesian rational procedure. In the zone which concerns it – beliefs about the self and its affective relations – it in effect requires total suspension of previous belief, much as Descartes had done. But the recovery of conviction follows, not the iron logical links of clear and distinctive ideas, but on the contrary, the slippery path of interpreted free-association. The central role of the notion of the Unconscious is to devalue, de-legitimate, disenfranchise all convictions:

inner compulsion and lucidity therefore constitutes no defence. If anything, it constitutes an aggravating and suspect circumstance. We believe what our Unconscious instructs us to believe, and we are not privy to its motives or reasons. This doctrine is applied primarily to beliefs about our own states of mind, but strictly speaking it should apply equally to all our beliefs without distinction.

What way is there, then, to true opinion and hence to sensible conduct? There is but one: to heed only those opinions that have been re-validated, checked, passed through the elaborate procedure for gaining entry to the Unconscious, and obliging it to disgorge its secrets.

So we leave the Cartesian rationalistic world in which knowledge is sovereign, and the world secondary, and where no cognitive hierarchy is permitted amongst men; and we re-enter a world in which a certain vision of the world is endowed with enormous authority, solidity, priority, and *it* is allowed to ascribe the appropriate standing to cognitive procedures and to inquirers. The general features of the world are taken as known and given: the standing and authority of cognitive claims and claimants follows *from it*. A fixed vision of the world engenders a fixed sacramental hierarchy in the world, ranking men into those who Know and save, and those who, if properly reverential, may receive salvation. The Freudians resemble the Marxists in their inversion of the principle that cognitive sovereignty is attributable *only* to rational *procedure* standing outside the world: sovereignty returns to a substantive conviction concerning the alleged dominant force *in* the world.

The notion of the Unconscious, with its immediate and crucial implication of the de-legitimation of all naturally held ideas, when left without benefit of endorsement by the appropriate hierarchy, is the principal device for the attainment of this end; but it is not the only one. The notion of the Unconscious is the equivalent of a doctrine of a kind of universal cognitive Original Sin. Those in deep sin are not fit to sit in judgement on their saviour.

Another important device is located in the nature of recognized evidence and its relation to theory. The gathering of evidence through 'free-association' ensures that the material is endlessly various and chaotic. It needs to be classified, 'interpreted', before it can be used at all in relation to explanatory schemata. The sheer polymorphousness of the data already introduces a large element of arbitrariness into classification/interpretation; but this volatility is reinforced by the much stressed principle that the material is cunningly offered so as to deceive, and that the deception can be extremely sophisticated and involve double-bluffs at any number of levels. Only the licensed Interpreter can unmask these multi-layered disguises. But he, in turn, is defined by his membership of the Guild, and by his commitment to its Doctrine.

There is nothing in the least unusual about such a world: most worlds which men have inhabited have satisfied this general formula. Inquiry was not allowed to overturn their comfort-giving world. From the viewpoint of a post-Cartesian rationalist, the construction of such a world is shamefully circular, a blatant case of begging all questions. But from the viewpoint of the faithful inhabitants of such a world, its own suspension – in the interest of external, independent scrutiny – could constitute a moral solecism. What is unusual, though perhaps not unique, about the Freudian world is that it is built up entirely out of naturalistic elements. In this way, as in some others, psychoanalysis really belongs to our age. Freud does indeed stand, as was claimed, at the culmination of the progression which leads from Copernicus via Darwin, a progression which established the naturalization of man, the definitive inclusion of man in Nature, and the refusal to grant him any extra-territorial status. The Unconscious is emphatically a naturalistic concept – which is an essential part of its appeal; but its role in the Freudian world-construction resembles precisely that of various transcendent realms present in earlier, non-naturalistic belief systems. A cosy, morally saturated, cognitively hierarchical, salvation-promising world is constructed; but its cognitively privileged realm, this time, seems to be provided by *nature*.

5
Ailments of Reason

Nature devours Reason

Reason imposed an orderly inquiry onto the world: this engendered a single Nature, unified by symmetrical laws. By the middle of the nineteenth century, and in particular after Darwin, it became obvious that the part of nature making the most impact on the image of man was *biology*. Darwin's unification of the biological world, and the inclusion of man in it, had underscored what others had argued on more formal grounds: that there is but one Nature, and man is part of it. But Darwin had also reminded us that Nature functions through conflict, aggression, and the elimination of the vanquished, and that the equipment which organisms develop serves primarily the survival of the organism and of the species to which it belongs.

From all this, one can reach the *general* form of the argument, which is quite sufficient for an irrationalist conclusion, and is independent of specific detail. It runs: orderly Reason engenders symmetrical Nature. Nature allows *no* exceptions or extra-territoriality for its creatures. But Reason is committed, *precisely*, to pretensions of such a kind. Therefore Reason must be a fraud, a spurious façade for something else. It is part of Nature and cannot claim to stand outside and above it. In its un-masked form, it becomes part of Nature – *and* loses its authority. So

Reason, having produced an all-embracing Nature, is thereby also deprived of its rank and authority within it.

More specific naturalistic theories are all of them *ex hypothesi* committed to a mild irrationalism of this kind; they may, but need not, also be irrationalist in a more extreme and virulent way. Having refused to grant Reason an extra-territorial status, thereby forcibly naturalizing it in this world and demoting it, they do not then all of them agree in the evaluation of the role of Reason within the world, and its further prospects. The values such theorists favour may be (as is the case with Marx and Freud) not too far removed from those which had enjoyed the support of rationalists proper. Reason may not be all it claimed to be, but what it proposed in the world may still be praiseworthy for intra-mundane reasons. Alternatively, however, a more vigorous irrationalism is also possible: it can be argued that the loss of extra-mundane authority deprives Reason of *all* authority, that all claims go by the board with the loss of the old pretensions. Reason not only claimed a spurious status, but what it did was positively harmful. This theme is certainly present in Nietzsche, and rather less so in Freud (in as far as it does not seem to affect Freud's own values, whether or not in all logic it should).

Pre-established Harmony returns

So the conclusions of these Naturalizations-of-man arguments need not *always* be irrationalist. There is a whole important sub-class of 'Naturalization of Man' theories, which avoid irrationalism by means of what in effect is a Providential Coincidence (or Pre-established Harmony) argument. Hegelianism was of course a very extreme case of such a view: at each historic stage, Reason revealed just about as much or as little as was required and appropriate at that time, as much as humanity was ready for at that stage, and she reserved her final and total self-revelation for the End. There it found Hegel himself, ready and waiting for it. Pragmatism, similarly, believes cognitive processes to be but a species of biological ones, but none the less this world is so well arranged that the processes help us make the very best of things, and so we are right to trust our own views, by and large. No need to opt out: knowledge and nature were made for each other, right from the start. It is not very clear how we could tell, or what we could do about it, if things were not so well arranged after all: we would be stuck with our misguided complacency, and unable to escape it even if it killed us. But Pragmatists seem to be men of sanguine temper and incurably optimistic, and they do not easily contemplate such a contingency. They also like to commend such a cheerful temper to all would-be thinkers.

The most distinguished and influential contemporary Pragmatist, W.V.O. Quine, emphatically commits himself to a position of this kind. He explicitly repudiates the Cartesian aspiration to Cosmic Exile (the excellent phrase is Quine's own). At any stage in the cognitive development of mankind (or, indeed, of all life), we can, it would seem, happily build on the existing inheritance, in the confident expectation that, though no doubt often mistaken in detail, in general outline it is sound and provides an adequate basis for further effort. In other words, the reasons which impelled Descartes to seek exile, the distrust of the cultural inheritance, are dismissed.[1] Cognitively speaking, all's well with the world. This is a premiss or a justification for a strategy or attitude which only works if that complacent, cheerful assumption is indeed correct. If it is not, how shall we ever discover it? We'll pay with our failure to recognize our mistake, but our demise may save us from having to face our error.

My own suspicion is that this distinctively pragmatist kind of confident optimism has distinctively American roots: the background vision embraces the social and economic history of North America, and the biological history of the species – but it has little sense of the long periods of stagnation and deadlock which characterize most other phases of human history. America was

[1] cf. W.V.O. Quine, *From a Logical Point of View* (Harvard University Press, Cambridge, MA, 1953); *Ontological Relativity and Other Essays* (Columbia University Press, New York and London, 1969).

born modern and progressive, it did not need to attain modernity, and Pragmatism is based on the assumption that the important truths are all there waiting to be found, as was the case in this happy period and, in a somewhat more brutal form, in biology. William James himself was a little wobbly as between the view that pragmatism was the truth for all, and that it was the distinctive expression of the American spirit.[1]

Harmony or siege

In general, we can distinguish between those Naturalizers, like Freud, who conclude that man must be redefined in consequence of his naturalization, and that Reason as a human faculty deserves less reverence than she has claimed; and those who, like the Pragmatists, joyfully acclaim our incorporation in Nature, but also think that Nature is so well arranged that she encourages sound rational habits anyway, so we have no need to disavow our previous commitment to Reason. They only say that Reason really is rather more at home in Nature than she had previously suspected. She has no need to seek Cosmic Exile: she is quite comfortable here; the habitat is benign, especially in America, and so we merely need to see Reason, and Nature, in a different light. She is no longer vindicated by her extra-natural status, but, on the contrary, by her comfortable, well-favoured and well-established place within Nature.

The Providentialists do of course lay themselves open to a charge of facile optimism and of blatant circularity of reasoning. In a world in which values are dictated by class interests, for instance, how very fortunate that Marx and Engels should be born at the very moment when the proletariat, emerging into self-consciousness, could formulate its own and ultimate human ideology through the mouths of those two renegade and highly typical sons of the bourgeoisie! Just think of it: had they been

---

[1] William James, *Pragmatism: A new name for some old ways of thinking* (Longmans, New York, 1907).

born at any earlier time, they would have been denied even a glimpse of the truth...

This is precisely the kind of thing that Providentialists in effect do claim. There is something comic about saying that, by a most fortunate coincidence, I happen to be standing at the one point in the world from which alone the world can be seen truly, or more generally, that the world is cognitively benign and ensures that we usually get it right. But comic or not, the circular device does enable Providentialists to remain Naturalizers, and yet to refrain from repudiating the name of Reason. Reason is the pawn of nature, but nature is so arranged that our reason tells us the truth about nature.

Cartesian Reason repudiated such circularity, and sought a genuinely independent foundation. It did not *assume* that cosmic arrangements are favourable to knowledge, and then say – carry on! It *worried* whether conditions were indeed benign.

Descartes *in the end* concluded that conditions were indeed benign: he entered into cognitive partnership with the deity. Extra-territorial reason guaranteed God, who then underwrote the intra-territorial applicability of reason. But Exile *was* necessary first. Reason had to go into the wilderness at the start, only to return with its cognitive Enabling Act.

There were good grounds for such a worry: in most historic circumstances, conditions were not at all favourable for the emergence of truth. Providentialists in effect claim that the circularity does not matter: the world is such a blessed place that their own particular circle contains the truth. But if it were not, how would they ever know? Their own circle of ideas precludes the possibility. But is it precluded *in fact*?

So we can distinguish between Providentialists, who believe in a Pre-established Harmony, and their opponents, who might be called Rationalists with a Siege Mentality. (Both are in a sense rationalists who have tried to come to terms with the naturalization of man, and so with the denial of dualism.) The latter do not allow themselves to be reassured by the complacent assumption of a pervasively benign world, which will look after us, at least in the end, or in some versions, all along the way. The Siege

Mentality assumes a world which is generally alien and hostile, or at best is neutral and totally unpredictable, and in which we cannot expect any cosmic underwriting and guarantee for our commitment to reason. For my own part, I happen to believe that the Siege Mentality is correct.

The old and new adversary

A central problem faced by Reason arises, as we have seen, from its incorporation in Nature. It then becomes but one agency or activity amongst others. At that point in the argument, the paths divide: either the laws to which nature is subject are so providentially beneficial that they ensure that Reason is to be trusted ('Providentialism'), or they are not.

On the latter assumption, we find ourselves in the presence of what is perhaps the main form of modern irrationalism. Its proponents differ from earlier critics of Reason in a most important respect: the attack is carried out, not in favour of a transcendent Authority, but in favour of some other force within the world which, they maintain, has a better claim on our loyalty (deep instinct, race, class, whatever). They do not, like Pascal, blame Descartes for managing without God. They blame him for failing to submit to Nature.

One of the main points to be made and stressed concerning the historic change in the Rationalism debate, as between the seventeenth and eighteenth centuries on the one hand and the nineteenth and twentieth centuries on the other, is this: during the earlier period, the debate took place, to put it in the simplest terms, between Reason and Religion. In the latter period, religion ceases to be the principal, or even an important, adversary. The crucial opponents of Reason, in modern times, are not those who claim that Reason must bow to the superior claims of an Authority which speaks from Above and Outside; they are those who insist that it must cede to a vital force *within* the world, and indeed one which derives both its vigour and its authority from its intra-mundane, natural status. If Nature is All, then legitimacy must be located within it.

There is, at the heart of modern irrationalism, a kind of intra-Nature chauvinism. The aliens from ontological foreign parts who used to govern us are to be driven out, like some cosmic Tarquins: from now on, only natives may aspire to rule – and the more indigenous, the better! The world for the mundane! All alien Pretenders are spurious. This replacement may be Will, class interest, instinctual adjustment...But the claim is then made that irrational forces are somehow *more* at home in this world, more truly part of it, than rational ones. Though Reason had established Nature, it has no real place in it, or only a subordinate one. This argument might be called the Suicide of Reason.

The impotence of Reason

This demotion of reason, by means of firmly locating it within Nature, constitutes one general form of modern irrationalism, in all its varieties. Providentialists share the irrationalist tendency to see Reason as one natural agency amongst others: but they evade the consequences. They mitigate the demotion. They do so by claiming that Reason, though not as independent and authoritative as had once been claimed, is nevertheless at least the properly commissioned agent of benevolent, respectable forces within nature which make for righteousness, whether cognitive or social or both. Deprived of independent authority, reason is credited with a power delegated by something greater and even more awe-inspiring. In fact, Providentialists more than merely mitigate the demotion of Reason; by linking or identifying it with a powerful tendency within Nature they endow it with an altogether new kind of dignity and authority. So Reason can, after all, be endorsed and trusted. It reveals the pervasive presence of benign forces, which in turn support and underwrite its own standing.

Modern irrationalism, or anti-rationalism, can, however, also assume quite another form. It need not proceed via naturalism. The basic argument can proceed, not via the naturalization of reason, but by way of a demonstration of the basic inability of reason to do that which she had set out to do. Not absorption into nature, but failure of performance, becomes the charge.

The absence of any guarantee of the validity or justifiability of rational method (whether or not equated with science) is one of the persistent themes of modern philosophy. The anxiety about the absence of some kind of legitimating charter for modern science has something paradoxical about it, in as far as the cognitive explosion since the seventeenth century has been, at any rate so far, conspicuously, visibly, dramatically successful. We appear to be anxious about the viability of a highly successful concern.

The anxiety takes a number of forms. For instance: the actual data available to us are fragmentary and exiguous. What warranty is there for extrapolating from them? In particular, why should the future reproduce the regularities of the past? Or again: what guarantee have we of the consistency or completeness of the calculi we employ? This worry appears to find confirmation in certain technical conclusions of mathematical logic: the programme which would have turned all mathematical reasoning into the simple implementation of innocuous, uncontentious logical principles, *cannot* be carried out. If rational inquiry involves procedures which it cannot justify, can it be rational?

The Impotence of Reason argument is, basically, that indeed procedures are involved, which cannot be justified, and that consequently, even if successful, they remain irrational. They fail to satisfy the Cartesian longing for self-validation.

There is a certain link between the Suicide and Impotence of Reason. Those preoccupied with the latter problem, when they despair of finding a proof which would validate rational procedure, tend to fall back on the fact that *we* – our minds, our tradition, our culture, or whatever – in fact operate that way. They fall back on facts about our practice or custom, for lack of ability to establish or demonstrate a norm. What is a naturalistic demotion of Reason in one context also turns up as a *faute-de-mieux* solution to the problem of impotence in another. Nature usurps the role of reason, or deputizes for reason on account of its failure – whichever way you care to look at it.

The vindication of inference

The irrationalism which is rooted in the Suicide of Reason argument, the view that nature is all-embracing and we should not strive to transcend its promptings, sometimes has what one might call a meaty or juicy quality: the irrationalist waxes lyrical in praise of the deep wisdom of the community or the tradition, of blood or soil or class, or the vibrant vigour of the dark inner forces of the psyche. The juiciness of the prose springs from the fact that he has some positive force to praise and adore. Irrationalists of this kind have often been masters of an eloquent literary style.

The Impotence of Reason argument, on the other hand, is rather less promising from the viewpoint of literary panache and fireworks. The trouble is that this kind of irrationalist does not arrive with some rival candidate of his own whom he favours and whose dark and mysterious powers he could praise in his song. All he does have, really, is the failure of one candidate, Reason, rather than the triumph of a rival. There are limits, perhaps, to the literary potential of *Schadenfreude*. Notwithstanding this handicap, some irrationalists in this tradition, notably P. Feyerabend, have done their best with such unpromising material.[1] Perhaps this only provides the poetry of irrationalist tantrums, feeble stuff when compared with their rivals, who celebrate the triumph of Nature, and rejoice in a splendid *Götterdämmerung* of Reason. But it does deserve comment.

One of the most important and interesting modern attempts at solving the problem of validation is Karl Popper's. Popper's earliest and still perhaps most famous work[2] is in effect a reinterpretation of science as such, a reinterpretation intended to be a

[1] cf. P. Feyerabend, *Against Method* (NLB, London, 1975).
[2] K.R. Popper, *The Logic of Scientific Discovery* (Hutchinson, London, 1959).

solution of Hume's problem. Popper hoped to succeed where Kant had failed: to vindicate the rationality of science, and save it from being demoted to a mere contingent custom of the human mind.

The argument he deployed was basically very simple. The whole of science, on his view, consists of nothing but the formulation of hypotheses, and of their successive elimination. Science is the elimination of theories by counter-example. The falsification of a generalization by a counter-example is, logically, a perfectly uncontentious procedure. The principle involved is simply that a well-established counter-example definitively establishes that the generalization is false. This is indeed a luminously self-authenticating principle. It would have warmed the heart of Descartes, who would have immediately recognized it as one of those lucid self-justifying truths which a rational mind cannot reject. It was principles such as these which were meant to help us escape from mere 'custom and example'. And, for Popper, it is *the* principle which enables us to escape into genuine knowledge, out of self-perpetuating, closed thought.

It can, in effect, be presented most plausibly as a direct lineal descendant of Descartes's *cogito* argument. What Descartes had in effect done was to say that only the immediate data of consciousness were indubitable, and un-amenable to the manipulations of the Daemon (alias culture). He called that indubitable base a substance of the self, but this was either a merely verbal adornment, or the addition of eminently dubitable metaphysics. Shorn of all this, it can then, in the Popperian version, be read (though Popper himself is no subjectivist) as follows: we have our immediate data base, and we are justified in inferring that anything incompatible with it is false. This principle has that luminous, self-validating authority which Descartes sought as a means of escape from error and mere contingent, culturally inspired opinion.

So in order to proceed and be rationally vindicated, science requires nothing but this one, uncontentious, lucid, cogent and self-justifying principle. So a clear and distinct idea is available, after all, and able to guide us. But it also needs those empirical data destined to act as falsifiers, as eliminators of theories. This will turn out to present a problem.

On this view, science no longer consists of a corpus of established truths: the only thing which is actually established is that a certain set of generalizations has been shown to be *false*. There is no body of generalizations known to be true; at most, one could say that among the infinity of as-yet-unfalsified ideas, there are some which are at present at the head of the queue. Some ideas are located in the front line, and have the honour to be most conspicuously subject to the test of fire by sustained attempts to falsify them.

How are these front-line heroes selected? It is at this point that Popper differs markedly from the previously conventional philosophies of science. It was often supposed that, from amongst the population of ideas not yet known to be either true or false, science should select those which seem most probable, which appear to have the best prospects of survival, given their past record. Popper is sceptical about the possibility of grading rival ideas in this manner; but above all, he insists that highly improbable ideas have just as good, or indeed a better, right to a place in the front line as the 'probable' ones. The greater the risk of falsification which attaches to an idea, and the more hostages it gives to empirical fortune, the greater also its content and value: the more we shall have discovered and attained if we test it, and the ordeal does *not* falsify it, if it survives unscathed. The greater the risk, the greater the gain in case of success, or rather in the avoidance of failure, and the greater the cognitive achievement, the greater the cognitive booty brought home.

Note that, on this account, the practice of science falls into two parts. One part evidently satisfies all the canons of Cartesian rationality: the principle of falsification by counter-example is manifestly uncontentious. It is not indebted to the prejudices of any one culture. It is rationally compelling for all Cartesian minds, willing to heed the voice of clear and distinct ideas. It makes them an offer they cannot refuse. One must also assume the existence of some empirical data (to act as eliminators). If these two elements are granted, then science can claim to be rational, and to be justified.

But there are also other activities, notably the discovery and formulation of ideas for testing, and perhaps their rank-ordering for subjection to testing. These activities are basically non-rational for Popper, and neither can, nor need, be endowed with a rational justification. There is no procedure of discovery, and discovery has no logic. Ideas can come in any old way, and the manner or order in which they arrive confers no privileges or priority on them. All one can say, in a loose way, is that it is good for a thinker to immerse himself in a problem; but neither immersion nor non-immersion constitutes any kind of guarantee of successful discovery.

This theory was intended to be a support for rationalism. It is indeed possible to construct a model of science along these lines. This model then contains no steps that need to be taken on trust. Ideas, theories, are fed in at one end and 'data' at the other; this input of ideas itself is not expected to satisfy any criteria of rationality to begin with, and so it cannot *fail* to satisfy them. But the confrontation of ideas and data follows the rules of an obvious, self-evident, lucid, and compelling logic. That *is* science. So science is rational. Q.E.D.

There is of course a price to pay: science must now be seen, not as the provider of reliable truths, but only as the reliable eliminator of falsehoods. There are no definitively established truths. These are only definitively established falsehoods. There always remains an infinite reservoir of as-yet-uneliminated ideas; and any discrimination we practise amongst these still surviving candidates is itself, once again, excluded from science proper, and from the requirement of rationality.

The idea of a concrete activity which conforms to such a recipe is not self-contradictory. No doubt there could be an institutionalized inquiry carried on strictly in this way. There could be an intellectual community devoted to the formulation of interesting ideas and their testing, and committed to the elimination of all ideas tested and found wanting. The community would have no rigid commitment to any set of ideas, though it could allow personal attachment by individual members for this or that theory – as long as it did not lead to any undue protection of the said theory from unprovable evidence.

But such an activity would bear only a rather distant relationship to the concrete activity actually recognized as science in our society. This consists of a corpus of doctrines which is not just an arbitrary sub-group of all as-yet-uneliminated ideas. It is, instead, a corpus either held to be true, or at any rate close enough to the truth to warrant the risking of lives and fortunes on it.

So the price paid for Popper's complete rationalization of a very pure science is that the practical aspect of science, and the confidence we have in the application of well-established ideas, whether of science or of common sense, are liable to be consigned to the irrational. It is very difficult to explain in what sense those beliefs are indeed rational: the assigning of numerical probabilities to entire hypotheses or theories has an exceedingly artificial air. A curious effect of Popper's attempt to save science for rationality is that whilst he succeeds in securing this for a 'pure' science, purified in accordance with his recipe, he does at the same time actually highlight the irrationality of our faith in the very extensive and important practical application of science, normally treated as an integral part of science.

This point is reinforced by another frequent criticism of Popper: even the rationalization of 'pure' science, its reduction to operations which are strictly and simply logical, hinges on the availability of 'hard' data, of unambiguous, externally and indubitably supplied 'facts'. But the kind of 'fact' which confirms or disconfirms very general theories is generally liable to diverse interpretations. Individual facts are 'theory-saturated', and any single recalcitrant fact can easily, like a captured spy, be 'turned around' and reinterpreted in a way which obliges it to conform to the theory. If this is so, the pretty and inspiring Popperian picture of the elimination of great theories by a single brave defiant fact turns out to be a myth. But if a single fact can do nothing, just how many forcibly 'converted', reinterpreted facts can a theory tolerate?

These two considerations are the main ways in which the Popperian enterprise has been criticized. They have led men working in the Popperian tradition, such as I. Lakatos and P. Feyerabend, to develop modifications which led, in the case of the latter thinker, to outright and brazen forms of irrationalism. Recognizing that very abstract scientific theories are not so much hypotheses which can stand or rather fall with a single counter-example, but constitute 'research programmes', that is, abstract schemata which inspire specific theories but which themselves do not face such direct confrontation with reality, Lakatos has developed a somewhat cumbersome set of criteria, intended to guide us to a rational appraisal of rival 'research programmes'.[1] The application of the criteria is liable to be a somewhat rough and ready matter. It is difficult, in the end, to see it as anything other than near-abandonment of the attempt at providing science with a rational basis.

In the case of Feyerabend, the irrationalism is open and avowed, and indeed deliberately and petulantly provocative. He enthusiastically adopts the slogan 'anything goes' to express the view that there are no rational cognitive procedures, and that all procedures and indeed conclusions are equally valid (or invalid). His exposition and demonstration of his view is based on the assumption that he has already demonstrated that indeed 'anything goes', so that all assertions, inferences, contradictions etc. are permissible, and hence that he, Feyerabend, can do no wrong. Once such a principle is at his disposal, and confers all cognitive liberties on him (though not, it seems, on his critics), it is of course very easy for Feyerabend to establish his own (or indeed any) conclusions. It is all a bit like Descartes in reverse. Descartes thought he had secured a divine underwriting for all of his own and distinct ideas (having used some of them to secure such a warrant), and then proceeded happily to use all his logical intuition. Feyerabend grants himself a universal warrant for any

[1] See, for instance, I. Lakatos, 'Falsification and the methodology of scientific research programmes', in *Criticism and the Growth of Knowledge*, ed. I. Lakatos and A. Musgrave (Cambridge University Press, Cambridge, 1970).

affirmation (because 'anything goes'), and with its help establishes – without much difficulty, not surprisingly – that the world of cognition corroborates all his own views. He has in effect invented a game at which he cannot lose.

Though the book itself is an absurd and somewhat hysterical exercise, carried out in a self-confessedly Dadaist style, it does contain a serious point: once one accepts the Popperian view that the rational element in science is the elimination rather than the substantiation of theories, that we cannot ever infer open-ended theories from data in our possession, it becomes very hard to endow our substantive convictions with any rational justification. It isn't so much that 'anything goes', as that it becomes difficult to explain why this should *not* be so.

6
Counter-Currents

Absolutism returns for pragmatic reasons

The much-renowned and highly influential work of Thomas
Kuhn resembles Popper's in one way at least: most certainly, it
was not written with any deliberate irrationalist intent.[1] Nevertheless it does have powerful, and widely exploited, irrationalist
implications. It also constitutes a firm specimen of an argument
also encountered elsewhere, in diverse terminologies, but with
the same central idea.

In one sense, Kuhn primarily attacks the individualist
mythology of science: the story, shared by Popperian and
pre-Popperian philosophy of science alike, and going back to
Descartes, of an *individual* inquirer facing data, and trying to
make sense of them in terms of a theory. The individualist
assumption is shared by 'inductivists', who suppose that this solitary hero assembles his data first, and *then* allows them to lead
him to a theory, and by their Popperian opponents, who present
the inquirer as first of all pulling a theory out of a hat, and *then*
bravely setting out to seek out the very data which could most
hurt it.

[1] cf. T. Kuhn, *The Structure of Scientific Revolutions* (2nd imp, University of
Chicago Press, Chicago, 1963).

It doesn't happen like that, asserts Kuhn. Researchers live in communities. They think in terms of a shared and presupposed picture, which Kuhn calls a 'paradigm'. They do not question paradigms: membership of the research community is defined by loyalty to the paradigm, and the ability and eagerness to fit data to the paradigm.

Why must this be so? Data are so manifold, chaotic and ambiguous, that if no paradigm were available and dominant, disagreement and chaos would be endemic. This is indeed the case, according to Kuhn's perceptive observations, amongst the pre-paradigmatic, and hence pre-scientific, social 'sciences'. It is only the order arbitrarily introduced by the paradigm, which limits the possibility of endless interpretative alternatives, and thereby makes orderly inquiry possible. It would not be possible to close these off by rational means. So it is done by the non-rational, authoritarian 'paradigm'. Only thus is cumulative, comparative work possible. The possibility of science depends on order, and not on liberty. Without the Paradigm-Sovereign, the life of ideas would be solitary, poor, nasty, brutish, and short. Only thanks to the peace established by the Paradigm can they in fact live, cooperate, and grow.

But is the Paradigm itself immortal then? What happens when it dies? Will it rule forever? Not so. The Paradigm must die. There comes a time when the Paradigm faces ever increasing and multiplying difficulties, which in the end overwhelm it. This is known as a Revolution, and it is terminated by the imposition of a new Paradigm. As at Nemi, the paradigm that slays its predecessor, weakened and declining in strength, secures the succession. The land will flourish again under a new and vigorous ruler. The paradigm is dead; long live the paradigm!

Kuhn reinforces his argument by the consideration, which indeed pervades his argument, that we cannot ever see reality directly, but *only* with the help of a paradigm. There is no direct, paradigm-free access to reality. Only the order imposed by a paradigm allows an observer to compare a proposition with the world, and decide whether or not the two tally. So our ideas never confront reality directly, but only through the mediation of a paradigm. But this being so, no paradigm as such can ever directly confront reality. (It would need another paradigm to do so...). The Sovereign can do no wrong: for it would take another Sovereign to make it so.

Kuhn goes on to insist, most plausibly, that paradigms are mutually 'incommensurate': there is no common idiom or measure in terms of which one paradigm could be compared with another. Modifications which can be presented in the same idiom, and which consequently can be rationally argued, remain, *ex hypothesi*, within the same paradigm. It is a shift to a new and incommensurate idiom which constitutes a revolution, a paradigm-shift. But this being so, such shifts, conceptual quantum leaps, to use the fashionable metaphor, cannot be rationally assessed.

This is inherently persuasive, and in any case follows from the contention that we can only apprehend reality through paradigms. The only possible shared idiom in terms of which paradigms could be compared and ranked in merit, would be reality itself: the paradigm closer to reality would then, naturally, be the better one. But such a comparison between paradigm and reality is excluded *ex hypothesi*: reality can only be apprehended *through* paradigms. This being so, no sense can be attached to declaring one paradigm better, truer, than another. This would require the comparison of a paradigm with paradigm-free reality. But we have no access to any such thing: paradigms have been declared to be the indispensable tool for the apprehension of reality. So inter-paradigmatic comparisons must themselves be consigned to the realm of the irrational. This is strictly parallel to the view that, if morality and legality is and can only be the will of the Sovereign, no sense can be attached to a moral or legal order prevailing *between* sovereign political units, and sitting in judgement *over* sovereigns. The argument for the absolute authority of political sovereigns is parallel to the argument for the authority of cognitive sovereigns, i.e. 'paradigms'. Authoritarianism is in the end accepted, as in Hobbes, not because it is divinely ordained, but because our mundane predicament requires it. This-worldly pragmatic considerations, rather than reverence for Revelation, leads us to absolutism.

Given this set of premisses, no escape is possible from the irrationalist conclusion. Kuhn personally appears to combine his vigorously formulated theory of incommensurate and hence sovereign paradigms with a firm belief in scientific progress – in other words with a conviction that later paradigms are after all better than earlier ones. There is of course no law to prevent an author from holding contradictory views, if he finds that psychologically he can do no other: but there is no logical way of squaring this optimistic faith with Kuhn's own central idea.

A position very similar to Kuhn's, though expressed in quite a different terminology, was adopted much earlier in this century by the philosopher-historian-archaeologist R.G. Collingwood.[1] He claimed that the questions asked in any given period of mankind's intellectual history only made sense against the background of the 'absolute presuppositions' of that age. These presuppositions themselves remained unquestionable – though they were not eternal, and were in due course replaced. Like Kuhn's Paradigms, to which they correspond rather closely, the succession of absolute presuppositions forms a progressive series, even although they are mutually incommensurate: for there simply is no third mediating idiom, in terms of which they could be compared and measured. In Collingwood's case, as in Kuhn's, the impasse is generated by the joint presence of two insights: the dependence of intellectual and cognitive activity on a socially sustained conceptual background, which is historic, contingent and temporary, *and* the conviction that, none the less, there is such a thing as scientific progress.

Kuhnian irrationalism – whether or not endorsed as such by Kuhn in person – with its invocation of the incommensurateness of successive scientific visions, is interesting and important in that it resembles and overlaps with another fashionable form of irrationalism, the mystique of incommensurate and self-sustaining *cultures*. The point, often made about cultures as allegedly non-comparable totalities, is applied by Kuhn to successive visions within science.

[1] R.G. Collingwood, *An Autobiography* (Oxford University Press, Oxford, 1939; repr. 1970).

The sovereignty of culture

One of the most influential philosophers of the twentieth century is Ludwig Wittgenstein. His particular version of irrationalism can perhaps best be approached through the intellectual situation in the last decades of the Habsburg empire, of which Wittgenstein was a somewhat eccentric, yet not altogether untypical, product.

In the Habsburg empire, there was a specially acute form of the conflict between what one might call the adherents of *Gesellschaft* (society) and of *Gemeinschaft* (community). The former term conveys the notion of an open society of anonymous individuals, related by contract rather than status, engaged in a free market both of goods and of ideas, freely pursuing their own aims, and having but a light and provisional commitment to cultural background, whether gastronomic, dialectal, sartorial or religious. In contrast with such liberalism, there was also a romantic mystique of a closed cultural community, whose members found fulfilment in its very idiosyncrasy and distinctiveness, and in the affectively suffused, highly personal even if hierarchical relationships which it sustained. This opposition pervades nineteenth- and twentieth-century thought, and was felt with special acuteness in Central and Eastern Europe.

There were good and obvious reasons why it was felt with special vigour in the poly-ethnic, socially mobile yet highly stratified and competitive Austro-Hungarian empire. Cosmopolitan, economically successful but ethnically uprooted and status-ambiguous individuals were drawn to liberalism, which had allowed them to rise and promised them acceptance; the adherents of the new ethnic nationalism were drawn to the romantic alternative, a return to a closed community, which would enforce protection not only of products, but above all of (ethnic) cultures. Each of the visions had its own quite distinct perception both of knowledge and of conduct. For the liberals, conduct was the pursuit of personally chosen aims by rational, instrumentally effective means; for the romantics, conduct was the playing out of a role within a larger, *communal* scenario, a role which contributed to the perpetuation of the whole community, which in turn conferred significance and value on the role and its carrier. For the liberals, knowledge was the free establishment of theories constrained by nothing other than the obligation to respect facts; for the romantics, real knowledge was a many-stranded activity, which played its part in the perpetuation of a living culture, its values, its hierarchy. It was not abstract and universal, but concrete and socially incarnate.

There is little evidence that Ludwig Wittgenstein was consciously and directly preoccupied with this confrontation, in its explicit, conventional, socio-political and cultural terms. It is most doubtful whether, in these terms, he ever gave it any thought. None the less, this confrontation provides the best, and probably the only, framework for a genuine understanding of his own most curious development. In his youth he was first an engineer and then, under the influence of further education in England, a logician. He was also, at a relatively modest level by professional standards of the time, a mathematician. When he became interested in problems of logic and of the foundations of mathematics, and hence in the relationship of language to reality, he developed a theory of language and of thought. This theory was meant to explain both how it was that language could refer to reality, and how mathematics was possible at all. The first achievement was explained by means of an alleged similarity of the structure of the world and of language, in other words by an 'echo' or 'mirror' theory of meaning. The second problem was solved by claiming that logic and mathematics were concerned only with the form, and not with the content, of thought. If logic and mathematics prejudged nothing about the world, about the referential *content* of our assertions, then the necessary *compulsive* nature of logical and mathematical proof became intelligible, and ceased to be a deep mystery. Mathematical truth was compulsive because it said nothing. Mathematical compulsion was thereby so to speak domesticated and rendered innocuous.

Note that the theory simply *assumed* that language was only concerned, in any serious way, with factual reference and formal inference, i.e. with something common to *all* men, irre-spective of their culture. Cultural idiosyncrasy had nothing to do with real thought or the essence of language. Unwittingly, the whole exercise was deeply Cartesian and individualistic: it was concerned with the constraints imposed on thought and language by logic and reality, independently of any culture, the influence of which was disregarded or dismissed. Once again, *custom and example* were consigned to the doghouse. When real thinkers meet, they communicate ideas, and they are not concerned with each other's intonations, hairstyles, tartans or club ties. That is the general picture. This wasn't argued, but simply assumed; a problem was to be solved which was simply formulated in such terms, which were not questioned.

This theory expressed, almost to perfection, the underlying intuitions of the partisans of *Gesellschaft*. Wittgenstein's early work did not *argue* those assumptions about thoughts, knowledge, and language, which pervaded the liberal-universalist tradition. It took them for granted. Real thought was concerned with a universally shared reality. Cultural idiosyncrasy constituted a kind of irrelevant distortion or noise, and it was brushed aside in his work with a single dismissive remark. There was, he taught, a universal form of thought and language, concerned with nothing but reflection of objective fact and the imposition of logical form. This universal pattern was captured by the notation of formal logic, as developed by Russell and Whitehead, and it was quite invariant. Cultural idiosyncrasies of natural languages were irrelevant accretions, and received little specific comment. They played no part in the real business of language or thought. The omissions and additions for which they were responsible were quietly discounted and compensated by speakers and listeners, when they conveyed or comprehended the real sense of an assertion. And even when, in the final part of his early book, Wittgenstein is concerned with the 'mystical', it is assumed to be invariant in all men. Culture is deprived of influence not only on our rational cognition, but equally, on our ineffable relation to existence.

Such was Wittgenstein's 'early', and subsequently discarded, vision.[1] Wittgenstein's world-wide influence, however, was attained not by these early views, which received only relatively modest and narrowly professional recognition, but by his later or 'mature' philosophy. If his early philosophy left no room for cultural idiosyncrasy, his later philosophy left room for nothing else. Cultural idiosyncrasy becomes King. On the later view, language users now did little but celebrate their linguistic communion, though they did so in a wide variety of context-bound ways. He had now dramatically inverted his own position. If Marx had stood Hegel on his head, and Nietzsche had done much the same to Schopenhauer, then Wittgenstein had the unusual distinction of standing *himself* on his own head, and acquiring great fame in the process.

As far as the formal and surface exposition of his philosophy goes, Wittgenstein was driven towards *Gemeinschaft* more by push than by pull. It was the internal inacceptability of the *gesellschaftliche* theory of language, which he had expounded with such comically total confidence in his youth, which led him to what he was sure was the *only* alternative. The availability of only two options was of course an essential premiss for the argument, which formed the real heart of his philosophical development.[2] If there are but two possible choices, and if one of them is shown to be wrong, then the other one inherits the earth.

The universalistic, symmetrical, purely referential, conceptually unified, atomistic theory of language was rejected for obscure and technical reasons. It just did not work, and it certainly proved impossible to relate the simple and elegant scheme it offered to the real practice of speech. But, hidden under the overt 'push' argument, away from the unacceptable alternative, there was also some positive attraction, a pull *towards* the option he in the end embraced. The repudiated theory of language was clearly located in the rationalist tradition, in as far as it

[1] L. Wittgenstein, *Tractatus Logico-Philosophicus*, tr. C.K. Ogden (1922; repr. 1923 with corrections).

[2] L. Wittgenstein, *Philosophical Investigations*, tr. G.E.M. Anscombe (Blackwell, Oxford, 1968). See B. Magee, *The Great Philosophers: An introduction to Western philosophy* (BBC Books, London, 1987), p. 343.

contained a clear promise that the relationship of language to the world was to be both explained and justified: our capacity to seize reality in words was not to be simply accepted and taken for granted but was to receive its charter, and Wittgenstein's *Tractatus* was meant to be that Charter. It declared itself to be both unquestionably valid *and* in the end beyond the reach of words and articulation. It was a strange Charter indeed, in as far as he who used it was sworn, on pain of having failed to understand it, to disavow it when he had completed its perusal: Wittgenstein declared its ideas both to be beyond all doubt *and* to be meaningless, and hence to be relinquished as such by all those who understood him. All the same, a Charter it was, for all its oddity. This option offered an irrationalist account of its own legitimacy.

The subsequently discovered and embraced alternative option held out no such promise of rational proof or vindication. Nothing was or could be either explained or justified: it could only be described and accepted. It could only be accepted as custom and example, as a 'form of life'. *Gemeinschaft* is self-justifying: it does not link itself to any Universal Transcendent. It is sufficient unto itself. It validates itself in all its idiosyncrasy, and above all in this idiosyncrasy.

At this point, Wittgenstein embraced another hypothesis, though he treated it as an established truth, not as a hunch, and built its acceptance into the implicit definitions of his system. He turned it into an immediate and inescapable corollary of his very definitions and procedural principles. His followers for a time treated it as an established truth and the basis of a putative philosophical revelation. The hypothesis was: the fascination which some men have felt for difficult and virtually unanswerable questions, the longing for an illumination and proof which would justify our basic practices (cognitive, moral, and other), springs simply from the appeal of that mistaken universalist-liberal theory of language, which Wittgenstein had just repudiated and unmasked as *the* fallacy underlying all previous philosophy! In effect, he projected his own, very idiosyncratic, development on the entire history of thought. So the recommendation to indulge in minute observation of the actual customary law of one's speech, and to accept it without further pursuit of either proof or general pattern, was also a recipe for a *cure* of philosophical bewilderment and anxiety. The philosophic or rationalist impulse towards proof or justification could never receive any satisfaction. Rationalism is a disease. There is no answer; only a cure for the temptation to ask the question. This is one of the most bizarre and extreme forms of irrationalism of our time.

Note that Wittgenstein reached this implicit cult of *Gemeinschaft* in a doubly indirect or oblique manner. First of all, it was done by the denial, the elimination of the supposedly single other alternative, rather than by some positive consideration. This is always a suspect procedure. There is no reason to accept the claim that only those two options, and no other ones, are available. Wittgenstein did not actually show or adduce any direct arguments to convince us that we did, could, or should live only within a cosy and self-justifying cocoon of conceptual custom, embodied in a given system of ordinary speech. He merely tried to force us through that door by insisting, without evidence, that only one other door was available, and that one other door must remain forever locked.

But more than this: he did not focus on *society* as such. He spoke of *language*. There is no evidence I know of to suggest that he ever directly applied his mind to the Society/Community opposition, which had such a powerful hold on the political and philosophical imagination of so many of his compatriots and contemporaries. But he must have unwittingly absorbed a sense of this great divide; and when the universalist/liberal model of language failed him, he turned to what was supposedly the only available alternative, and one which appeared to be waiting in the wings. He then sold his followers a Closed-Community ethos, though not under that name, but packaged as an alleged revolutionary perception of the true nature of language. This vision also contained, he claimed, without ever securing the slightest supporting evidence, a recipe for 'dissolving' all philosophical problems (i.e. all problems concerning validation of the principles we employ in our diverse activities). If it were indeed true that the closed and idiosyncratic community is conceptually sovereign, final, self-sufficient, then indeed such a conclusion would follow. Return to your custom and totem, for there you'll find the only validation that can ever be given unto you. This strange socio-political doctrine, formulated *mit ein bisschen anderen Worten* [in rather different words], was proposed under the camouflage of a theory of language. So a vision of society is smuggled in on the coat-tails of a theory of language. *Gemeinschaft* prevails by default: no trans-communal, universally rational form of thought is possible.

If this be so, then all philosophical problems are solved at one fell swoop: in their speech habits, which include the evaluation of truth and falsehood, goodness and badness, beauty and ugliness, men inescapably and above all *properly* prejudge the answer to philosophical problems. If the conceptual or verbal custom by which they do so is indeed self-justifying, and constitutes the only vindication that it is ever possible to attain – well then, let us study our own verbal custom, and accept its implicit verdicts.

So *Gemeinschaft* was not commended directly: Wittgenstein never actually said that the Viennese should leave their megalopolis and return to a Tyrolean village or a Balkan *zadruga* or the *Staedtl*, or go off to a kolkhoz or a kibbutz; he never commended the wearing of lederhosen or the dancing of the *hora*. He was never quite so specific or direct. What he did do was tell Viennese, Cambridge, and other intellectuals, whose actual conceptual life was inevitably far closer to the model of *Gesellschaft* than to *Gemeinschaft*, that when they faced the legitimation crises of their own practices, when, for instance, they sought (misguidedly) the validation of mathematical or empirical or moral inference, they should comport themselves *as if* they were members of some Closed Community, untouched by centuries of the pursuit of norms which were to be trans-ethnic and trans-cultural, and whose authority was not merely that of the clan totem. They should treat their own custom as ultimate. A Cartesian civilization which had, for centuries, lived by a sustained critique of mere *custom and example*, was advised to embrace the doctrine that there was and could be no other kind of vindication under the sun. He received a rapturous hearing, notably in Oxford, and was for a time hailed as the final demystification, self-realization, and culmination of philosophy.

As an account of the languages of primitive man, prior to literacy, or the emergence of an elaborate division of labour, or of doctrinal theology and conceptual centralization, this is not at all bad, though this is not how it was presented; so, without intending it, Wittgenstein had turned himself into quite a good theoretical anthropologist. His disastrous mistake was to extend this account to *all* linguistic and conceptual systems, including notably modern ones, such as his own. If Wittgenstein were right, then the great achievement, or the terrible predicament – it depends on whether you are a positivist or a romantic – of *Gesellschaft* had never really happened. It did not happen because it *could not* happen. We all lived in *Gemeinschaften*, whether we knew it or not, because the very nature of language allowed us nothing else; so we could never live anywhere else. The intellectual turbulence experienced by Western man since the seventeenth century, and relived in acute and stressful ethnic/cultural terms in fin-de-siècle Austria, was – it turned out – about nothing at all. At most, about a misunderstanding of language!

In effect, Wittgenstein's programme recommended a collective infantile regression for all mankind. The primitive functional community, to which one was by implication advised to return under his guidance, would then, from its own resources, solve or rather 'dissolve' all the problems which had been engendered by the mysterious and misguided striving for a universal and philosophically justified way of thought. A proper theory of language allowed only *Gemeinschaft*. Therefore, we may, indeed we must, behave as if we were part of a *Gemeinschaft*, and our concepts and cognitive procedures had and would have no other foundation: this *must* be the case, for a correct understanding of language had shown that only *Gemeinschaft* is possible. *Custom and example* are sovereign after all. They must be, for no rivals are available, or ever can be.

Creativity through constraint

Noam Chomsky's theories of language are as influential as Wittgenstein's, and radically opposed to them, though this latter point has not yet been widely noticed. The ideas of the two thinkers have operated at such different levels that their confrontation has been much delayed, though it may yet come about.[1]

The basic difference is this: Wittgenstein's romanticism treats individual language systems, and above all the unreflective competence of their speakers, on which these languages are based, as given, final, self-explanatory, self-justifying – *terminal*. Attempts at explaining or justifying this competence are actually proscribed. That is indeed the main actual point he wishes to make. Cultures, 'forms of life', can, as he insists so emphatically, be neither justified nor explained. They can only be *described*. It is this sovereignty of custom and community, of 'custom and example' as Descartes had once put it, which constitutes Wittgenstein's romanticism, and the omnibus answers that his theory offers for philosophical problems.

Chomsky's achievement lies not so much in his solutions, which seem to be technical, volatile, and contentious, as in his astonishingly lucid and clear perception of a problem which others had at best only obscurely sensed, or had ignored altogether. Human speech is amazingly disciplined, rule-bound, and rich, and it observes rules of which the speakers are, in the vast majority of cases, wholly ignorant. The range of things we can articulate and comprehend is astonishing, and the possession of this infinite reservoir of meanings and comprehension calls for explanation. Language has its reasons of which the mind knows nothing.

---

[1] For general implications of Chomsky's ideas, see for instance his *Knowledge of Language: Its nature, origin and use* (Praeger, New York, 1986); *Language and Responsibility* (Harvester, Brighton, 1979); *Reflections on Language* (Temple Smith, London, 1976); and F. d'Agostino, *Chomsky's System of Ideas* (Clarendon Press, Oxford, 1986).

In a sense, Chomsky's views are an extension and continuation of Durkheim's critique of empiricism (though Chomsky does not seem to have been in any way influenced by Durkheim). It is the compulsiveness and discipline of our verbal behaviour which are so very striking. This can in no way be explained by empiricist principles of 'association'. These could only lead to some kind of agglutinative chaos, to the snowballing of meanings and associations in semantically unusable (because unrestrained) bundles. An acute awareness of the inadequacy of the associationist, empiricist account of our competence and discipline is something shared by the two thinkers. An associationist world would be much worse than an Expanding Universe: growing at an uncontrollable and ever-increasing rate, in all directions at once. We should all of us be suffering from a galloping semantic cancer. This expansion in one mind would not resemble that in another, and we would never be able to say anything to each other, or even to leave notes for ourselves. I might never be able to understand in the morning a note I had left for myself the previous night.

The remarkable verbal order which in fact does obtain, Chomsky argues, can only be explained on the assumption of a pre-programmed equipment, which can help us learn the features of a specific language only because its formal features, shared with other languages, are already anticipated, and limit the options available to the user and learner of the language. What we learn from experience is not the full rich picture with which we end; experience merely consists of nudges which activate a picture ready and waiting to be called forth – and experience also supplies the contingent tokens which the picture employs. Chomsky has gone beyond Durkheim, whilst unwittingly implementing some of his insights: Durkheim, following Kant, only noted the compulsiveness of certain central, as it were dominant, 'categorial' concepts. Minor concepts, the rank and file of our conceptual army, he seemed apparently to be quite willing to leave to the empiricists and to their associationist principles. It was only the cardinal concepts, which organized and dominated all others, which, in Durkheim's view, needed the help of ritual, so as to be instilled in our minds, and endowed with that disciplined compulsiveness which enables us to think, communicate, and become social and human.

By contrast, Chomsky's point about the disciplined nature of our linguistic comportment in no way distinguished between important and trivial words: it covers them all, without distinction of status. All our concepts, and not just the fundamental *Ordners* or organizers, are compulsively disciplined. Language itself is a kind of diffused ritual. We are somehow naturally inclined to observe and obey the imperatives of grammar; and Chomsky, as far as I know, offers us no explanation of our invaluable docility, but contents himself with trying to map its general forms and show that it cannot be acquired by 'association'. This distinguishes him from Durkheim, whose concern was primarily with the manner in which we are cowed into rationality, i.e. into orderly conceptual thoughts.

Chomsky invokes not merely our syntactical discipline, but also our conceptual richness, and he relates the two to each other. It is the fabulous number of things that we can say and apprehend, many of them quite original and highly complex, which highlights the impossibility of explaining our linguistic competence by the invocation of mere association, or by the mere recollection of prior examples. Language is not just a ritual, but a ritual which makes a modular use of limited equipment, so as to produce an infinity of articulable and intelligible assertions. This syntactic discipline engenders a world of astonishing richness *and* order, which the freedom of 'association' could never possibly have produced. Language seems to illustrate the favourite principle of authoritarianism: it is discipline which makes us truly free. It is this use of finite means for the production and comprehension of an infinite range of messages which is the central mystery of language. And it must be assumed that it is only *because* we are so astonishingly disciplined that we can systematically combine a rather restricted set of phonetic elements in such a fantastically wide and creative way. Freedom lies in the recognition of syntactical necessity.

As far as I know, no really adequate discussion of the

irrationalist implications of all this is available. In the simplest terms, however, the argument must run something as follows. We mainly, or exclusively, think through language; but if our speech is bound by deep rules of which we know nothing (and the unravelling of which is the object of linguists' inquiries which are arduous and highly contentious), then it would seem that we are not and cannot be in control of our own thought. Georg Lichtenberg had sensed all this when he said that we ought not to say 'I think', but only 'it thinks'. Chomsky has endowed Lichtenberg's aphorism with a precise content. *It thinks* deals a body blow to Cartesian rationalism at its very starting point: thought no longer engenders an autonomous self. The idea with which Cartesian rationalism starts right at the beginning, as its first premiss, is misguided. It simply is not true that 'I think'. *It* thinks. (The conclusion still follows: therefore it exists.)

Chomsky's own attitude to the problem thrown up by his own ideas seems to be one of half-grateful, half-resigned acceptance. It is *because* we are so rigidly structured that we have access to such a fantastic range of possible meanings. Hence it is our pre-wiring which enables us to be so unbelievably creative and original. So we ought not to resent our pre-wiring (or not too much?); we do, after all, owe it so much. At the same time, Chomsky also recognizes that pre-wiring seems to imply that there are some limits to our thought, and has on occasion indulged in the speculation concerning whether, for instance, the failure of psychology to produce significant results may not be due to the fact that our minds are so constructed that psychological problems are intractable for us.

What does seem obvious is that in the rhythm of our thought we follow underlying linguistic rules of which most of us are almost wholly ignorant. To this extent, we do inevitably violate the first rule of any Cartesian rationalism – to deploy only principles which are translucently intelligible to us, *and* cogent, and seen to be such. In fact, we generally have not the slightest idea what these principles are; hence we have no way of even asking ourselves whether they are sound, let alone of deciding, in

the interest of satisfying Descartes's principles of human rationality, whether they are luminously self-justifying.

On the other hand, the hope might be expressed that these
deep hidden syntactical rules govern only linguistic form, and not
the actual content and logical connectedness of what we say. This
is certainly a hope, though not one which strikes me as persuasive. It might be that the formal rules of Aristotelian or modern
logic are independent of any one language and can be translated
into all of them, and that inferences in any language can be
checked against it.

It is, however, not at all obvious that this is indeed so. The view
that the syntax of our language predetermines our metaphysics
has often been propounded. The idea is anything but absurd,
though it has never been worked out with any precision. Can it be
that our speech, which we follow without understanding it, does
not affect the content of our thought? Do we not rely, for our
substantive conclusions, on linguistic rules to which we have
no access, and whose soundness and authority we have never
scrutinized?

There is certainly a *prima facie* case for the irrationality of an
activity – verbal thought – which deploys principles of which the
practitioner is unaware, and which he has never scrutinized or
checked, and which he would not check because in any case
he does not understand them. When the insight connected with
the Chomsky revolution in linguistics confronts the Cartesian
ideal of thought, which allows itself to move only in the light of
principles which are clear to itself and luminously cogent, it is
hard to escape an irrationalist conclusion. Perhaps the irrationalist potential of this argument can be kept in bounds by various
considerations – such as, that the syntactical rules investigated by
linguists are neutral with respect to the logical rules governing
inference and compatible with them, so that the content of our
thought is not affected by the so to speak heteronomous nature of
language. The question deserves more investigation than it has in
fact hitherto received.

Treason most foul

A somewhat bizarre but significant book appeared between the wars: Julien Benda's *La Trahison des clercs*.[1] The suggestion that intellectuals are inherently traitors to something – whatever it be – has a powerful appeal: it is hard not to feel that there is something in it. The book is of some importance not merely because it bestowed what is probably an immortal phrase upon mankind. It is a passionately pro-rationalist book, written in an age when Reason was not faring at all well at the polls, so to speak, though the pleading of its case in the book is carried on in a somewhat perverse manner. Though few have noted it, the book commits treason of the intellectuals in the very act of denouncing it.

Benda argues that intellectuals should uphold eternal values and verities, and not go whoring after particular local identities, passions, interests, and cults. So far so good. The picture presented is simple and, as such, attractive. On one side, eternal verities, and on the other, special interests or passions. The line-up seems clear enough. Once upon a time, clerics – especially in the old days when they were, literally, clerics – were international and trans-ethnic, and in principle free of local attachments. The shedding of such bonds was then a formal professional obligation. They spurned particularistic totem poles, and they served abstract and universal ideas and ideals. For some reason, a corruption set in or accelerated during the nineteenth century and became accentuated in the twentieth: intellectuals brazenly identify with national or class or other special interests, and indeed they made a virtue of such identification. *Commitment* in the end replaces *proof* as the legitimation of assent. Benda roundly denounces them for this collective treason.

Benda wrote well before the coming of the overt fad of *commitment*, but what he says is highly relevant to it. Note that what is at issue is not merely lending one's support to this cause or that, one

[1] Julien Benda, *La Trahison des clercs* (Grasset, Paris, 1927).

party or another. That is a relatively superficial matter, and might even be justified within Benda's scheme by saying that on occasion, one party does indeed defend truth against falsehood. The really profound treason of the clerics consists of saying that *inherently* truth is linked to racial, class, or other mundane interests. *Commitment* as such is praised, rather than impartiality. Pragmatists, Marxists, Nietzscheans and others have indeed said as much. Existentialists turned it into their central doctrine. Proofs no longer being available, or being spurned as somehow demeaning and sordid, were replaced by the cult of gratuitous, even arbitrary *identification*. Cartesian rationalism urged us to identify with what we could prove, and the self was valued because it provided the most cogent premiss. The Existentialists taught that our identity was binding because it lacked proof, and that 'authentic' identity required this. Identity replaced proof.

Benda did for the rationalist tradition what romantics proper had done for the intimate organic community. The romantics had complained that the earthy common sense and gut loyalty, rooted in blood and earth, permeating the old community, had been abandoned by those seduced by the appeal of a bloodless, rootless rationalist cosmopolitanism. Benda has turned the tables and thrown back the charge of treason. In the traditional world, divines had no country: it was they, not proletarians, who had no nation, and they should be proud of it. Why do they scream about it now? The book no doubt deserves the success which it had.

One thing, however, should make one a little suspicious of the logic of this book. Many of Benda's arguments for a return by the intellectuals to their allegedly rightful stance and position are themselves curiously but persistently pragmatic in character. It would be better for us all if only the intellectuals did not encourage strife by identifying with worldly forces, he says. Well, perhaps it would. But can such an appeal to worldly advantage really claim to be an appeal to an eternal verity?

The really basic point is this. Benda does not adequately consider the possibility that those who abandoned the posture of representing universal and eternal truths, and opted for various forms of particularism, did so not because they were corrupt and bribable but for the very opposite reason: the inescapable human involvement in the earthy, earth-bound limitation, seemed *true* to them. They were sensitive to the *rational* argument that no other truth is ever genuine, and mundane bondage is the only kind of truth available to us. It is the only kind which gives us real satisfaction, which corresponds to our nature. It was, precisely, their effective commitment to rational thought, which led them to irrationalist conclusions. It was their rationality which led them to irrationalism. They felt morally bound to put their conclusions on record, because that was where reason had led them. If the conclusion were unpalatable, too bad. The really important and persuasive attacks on reason, on universalism, on rational order, were carried out by rational means, by reason itself. Some of the greatest irrationalists were perhaps despairing, tormented, but above all, *honest* rationalists in their own thought style. Benda commends Reason from the viewpoint of pragmatic consideration; they, on the other hand, commended Unreason for rational ones. Who is the traitor?

They did what they did because reason had impelled them to the conclusions which they reached. They recorded the facts of the case as they saw them. They often reached their position in anguish, knowing full well that they were devouring their own innards. Reason engendered Nature, and within Nature there is no place for Reason. Rational examination of man shows him up as merely an accumulation of perceptions (Hume), or to be part of nature (Nietzsche); either account leads, by altogether different paths, to the conclusion that what man calls Reason is but an activity at the service of non-reason. The suicide of reason was announced and preached by people who were, by temperament, honest thinkers. When Hume or Nietzsche say (in quite different senses) that reason is and ought to be the slave of passion, they say it *for good and honest reasons*. They would be committing genuine *trahison* if they *failed* to say it. In a remarkable footnote, Benda comes close to seeing this: whilst he continues to castigate Nietzsche's views, he admits that in his life, Nietzsche's devotion to ideas was remarkable. But there is more to it than that: Nietzsche reached his irrationalist conclusions by applying those very rationalist values which Benda commends.

The rationalism of Benda exemplifies an uncritical acceptance of a certain picture (abstract values *v.* particular interests). It indulges in the surreptitious but persistent invocation of practical advantage. The most interesting examples of the tendencies which he condemned were really tormented cases of reason turning in on itself and devouring itself. This is an essential part of the story.

Checklist of Reason-bashing

A brief list of attacks on reason may be useful. Many of them have been discussed at greater length, in context, in the course of our exposition. In this section, we are only concerned with a kind of catalogue or index of irrationalisms. These anti-rationalisms will be presented in a summary way, which aims only at their identification, rather than any proper exploration. The names cited are not necessarily of thinkers who themselves wish to be irrationalists, or could fairly be so characterized. Their inclusion indicates no more than that their ideas can be used as parts of an irrationalist argument, not that they themselves endorsed irrationalist conclusions.

1   The argument from Popper, followed out to its limit by P. Feyerabend: if there is no way of assessing the merit of rival views when they are all compatible with the data as yet available (in an extreme version: no way of ranking any theories at all), no rationality can be attributed either to beliefs or to conduct.

2   Argument from regress: the first premiss of any procedure cannot, *ex hypothesi*, have a logically prior reason which would justify it in turn. Ergo, in the end, all convictions are but 'leaps', and all leaps equally irrational.

3   The Collingwood-Kuhn argument: if science can only work under the guidance of 'absolute presuppositions' or 'paradigms' which themselves cannot be examined or compared, science is irrational. If the absolute presuppositions or paradigms are incommensurate, there being no common idiom, there is hardly any sense in which such choice could be 'rational'.

4   The Schopenhauer-Nietzsche-Freud argument: if our conduct and thought are governed by a dark force which does not reveal itself to those it dominates, but on the contrary has great powers of deceit, rational conduct is difficult, to say the least. (In the Freudian version, it becomes possible if aided by a theory and technique which lays bare the *modus operandi* of those forces – but the theory and technique themselves are highly suspect.)

5   The argument from Hume: there is no rational way of validating aims or values. (Note that the conjunction of this point and the preceding one is far more powerful than either on its own. If our 'passions' are arbitrary but mild and so to speak sensible, as Hume thought, it matters little if they are beyond the reach of justification. If our passions are dark, devious, powerful, and turbulent, but our values may stand – which, strangely, was Freud's actual attitude – then we may, with luck and effort, do something. But if *both* points are valid, if the seas are turbulent *and* we have neither rudder nor compass...)

6   The argument from Wittgenstein: the old model of instrumental rationality, or of consistency of conduct, assumed a single universe of discourse, within which efficiency or consistency were possible. If, however, our sensibility to the world is invariably mediated by a whole number of autonomous 'language games', each

with its own autonomous rules, then there is no such single realm.[1]

7 The quite different premiss concerning language, provided by Chomsky. If our verbal thought is governed by principles not normally accessible to consciousness, it is hard to see how we could scrutinize the rationality of our own thought. A similar point can also be made differently, in terms of the so-called Whorf-Sapir hypothesis, which suggests that each language or group of languages imposes its own vision of the world on those who use it.

8 The so-called Duhem problem: if our ideas form an interconnected unity, can there be a non-arbitrary way of correcting error? *Any* part of the system may be responsible for a failure which occurs at any given point, and there is no way of identifying it.

9 The holistic-romantic conception of society: if human societies or traditions are complex but seamless and subtle unities, then perhaps they are not amenable to clearly calculated interference, guided by unique criteria and by a selection of means in terms of cost-effectiveness. They can only be guided by persons deeply immersed in the said traditions and responsive to the intimations they engender. A view of this kind can be found, for instance, in the work of the late Michael Oakeshott.[2]

10 A quite un-romantic variant of this argument can be developed specifically with regard to modern societies,

---

[1] The point about what Wittgenstein calls 'language games' is that they are autonomous sub-systems of language, and governed by its own criteria, not subject to any overall shared principle. This doctrine is crucial for Wittgensteinian irrationalism.

[2] cf. M. Oakeshott, *Rationalism in Politics and Other Essays* (Methuen, London, 1962).

given their scale, complexity, and extremely rapid rate of change. Rational assessment was possible in relatively stable societies, where most things were being held constant, so to speak, so that changes could be isolated and assessed. When everything changes at once, situations never really repeat themselves, and there is no way of 'learning from experience'.

11   Even more specifically, one can argue from the rate of change and the manipulability of our aims and values. Utilitarian moral theory accepted Hume's view to the effect that values were beyond proof, but it was untroubled by this, because it used actual human preferences as a kind of datum. If, however, our aims themselves are as it were *sub judice* and manipulable, where can a philosophy based on human preferences possibly find its premisses?

12   The incommensurability of values. This is a theme prominent, for instance, in the thought of Sir Isaiah Berlin.[1] The incommensurate plurality of values is, for him, a central premiss of liberalism. If that is so, it is hard to see, however, in what sense policy could ever be rational, any more than accountancy would be possible if it were to be carried out simultaneously in a number of mutually inconvertible currencies.

There is no suggestion here that this list is complete.

[1] I. Berlin, *Four Essays on Liberty* (Oxford University Press, Oxford, 1968).

7
Rationality as a Way of Life

Reason is not merely the name of a supposed path to the discovery of truth or the legitimation of principles. It is also a life-style. The two aspects are intimately connected. The thinkers who theorized about the nature of this alleged inner cognitive and moral guide, the repository of our identity, were also, in effect, knowingly or otherwise, codifying the rules of comportment of a newly emerging civilization, one based on symmetry, order, equal treatment of claims and of evidence. They were helping to bring about such a civilization. Rationality became a powerful philosophical ideal in a world which was also becoming rationalized by other agencies. The universal validity which philosophers credited to their discoveries was perhaps illusory. Instead, they were perhaps drawing up the Charter, or formulating the Constitutional base, of one social order among others. But it was a very special one. The unique civilization whose foundations they were laying down was in some way or other more rational than all the others. In what way? What exactly is rationalism as a life-style?

A rational person is methodical and precise. He is tidy and orderly, above all in thought. He does not raise his voice, his tone is steady and equal; that goes for his feelings as well as his voice. He separates all separable issues, and deals with them one at a time. By so doing, he avoids muddling up issues and conflating distinct criteria. He treats like cases alike, subjecting them to impartial and stable criteria, and an absence of caprice and arbitrariness pervades his thought and conduct. He methodically augments his capital, cognitive as well as financial. He ploughs back his profits rather than turning them into pleasure, power, or status. His life is a progression of achievement, rather than the static occupancy, enjoyment, and fulfilment of an ascribed status.

The obverse of his avoidance of the arbitrary is the possession of good reasons for what he does and thinks. The requirement of good reasons reinforces orderliness of conduct: if a reason is cogent, it must also apply in all like cases. The insistence on reasons is antithetical both to the acceptance of authority and of arbitrary, ecstatic revelation. Authority unjustified by reason is tyranny, and when supported by reason, it is in a way redundant. Reason alone should suffice. The man of reason ideally needs no additional incentives when the reasons are good. When good reasons are lacking, he does not allow mere rhetoric or ritual theatre to cow him. He is both restrained and self-governing. He is loth to join a multitude in committing folly.

The requirement of rational justification is extended to all life. The reasons themselves must be systematized. The separation of issues leads to the simplification of the criteria of success in any single activity. That in turn, in conjunction with the desacralization of procedures and methods, leads to a habitual, precise, and painstaking assessment of cost-effectiveness, and so to instrumental efficiency. Innovation when beneficial is adopted without undue inhibition. No sacred boundary demarcation of activities hampers its implementation. All of this supports and dovetails with an orderly division of labour, and makes possible a rational accountancy of success and failure. The free, untrammelled choice of means is encouraged both by the clear specification of aims and by the levelling out of the world: all things are equally sacred or equally profane, and so there are no sacred prescriptions or proscriptions to inhibit the choice of methods. They become subject to considerations of efficiency.

Dealings between men are similarly rational, guided by the free choice of clear ends by both partners, and by the coolly assessed advantages inherent in any bargain between them. Contractual relations replace those based on status. Society as a totality comes to be seen in the same light. Its organization is not *given*, but determined by rational contract. It is but the summation of free and rational contracts, entered upon by free and rational individuals.

In recent centuries, such styles of conduct have become more common and pervasive, and eventually dominant. They have come to be prominent in production, in cognition, in politics, in private life, and in culture. Their impact in these various spheres has not been identical: rationality is not applicable in the same way to all problems and activities. Philosophers have explored the principles and merits of rationality. Sociologists, impressed or appalled by the creeping and pervasive advances of rationality, and by its conquest of social life, have tried to understand the underlying social mechanics of this process. It is important to bring the ideas of the philosophers and the sociologists on this topic together. They constitute two aspects of what is but a single story.

The sociologist who, more than any other, is linked to the attempt to map and comprehend this creeping and pervasive rationality, is Max Weber. We have already sketched out his approach earlier, in the imaginary dialogue between Descartes and modern sociology: Durkheim on his own was incapable of answering Descartes's rebuttals, but was enabled to do so thanks to Weber's assistance. Weber fully perceived the uniqueness and distinctiveness of a rationality-pervaded civilization, and the manner in which it constituted a break with the principles normally governing agrarian societies. He saw its emergence as a mystery which required explanation. Unlike the providentialist Hegelo-Marxists, who saw the emergence of our particular world, with all its qualities, as the manifest destiny of all mankind, as an inherent continuation and culmination of a long and universal development, bound to arise sooner or later whatever happened, Weber saw it as the contingent, fortuitous event in the life of a particular religious tradition, which was its necessary (though not sufficient) condition. Durkheim saw communalistic ritual as the progenitor of the pan-human rationality of conceptual thought; Weber saw puritanical monotheistic nomocratic religion as the progenitor of orderly, symmetrical rationality, which alone makes a modern economy and science possible.

As with so many other thinkers, Weber's importance lies at least as much in the problem he highlighted, as in the solution he has proposed for it. The debate concerning the merit of Weber's partially religious account of the initially gradual, but eventually dramatic, spread of rationality has long been vigorous. It is unlikely to be settled soon. It may not be settled ever.

Economy One: production

The sphere of production is one of those in which the expansion, or blight, of rationality has received most attention, both from its admirers and its detractors. To some, the essence of the formula seems to be simple: the clear formulation of aims (namely, perpetual accumulation, which is, according to Marx, the Moses and Prophets of capitalism) and the ruthless and efficient choice of means. Human beings, human labour, are amongst those means. Their work is treated like a commodity. It is deployed in isolation from the part that is the work of a person and part of his life. It is just this indifference which makes it possible to make work instrumentally effective, and it is of course also one of the principal charges against the 'rational' capitalist productive system.

The social ruthlessness in the choice of means is complemented by a similar ruthlessness in the cognitive exploration of the world. We go where the wind of argument and evidence drives us. The vision of the world ceases to be socially constrained: *anything* can be the case, if evidence points that way. Things lose their elective affinities, and their connections are subject to evidence alone, and the verdict of evidence may not be prejudged. This sovereignty of brute fact engenders a socially icy world and a powerful technology, which enables the new system to deliver an unprecedented cornucopia of goods.

The entire system is contrasted with the traditional order, where the choice of methods was dictated by custom, and the choice of personnel was determined by status, so that work 'meant' something to the person carrying it out. What he did was linked to his identity and his personal relations. Likewise, conviction was linked to the social and natural orders: a stable social hierarchy simultaneously served both human and productive requirements, it did not permit their separation, and it was underwritten by the vision of nature. Productivity increased when the traditional order had lost its authority – so the liberal argument runs; constraints on choice of means had been removed, or at least diminished, permitting the untrammelled deployment of whatever method was found to be most effective. The new order also allowed the use of labour power if and when required, subject only to free contract, without further restrictive conditions, without any respect for 'human' relations, other than productive ones. The Romans considered a slave to be a 'speaking tool': rationality in production turns the worker into something similar. The difference is that now it is labour, and not the labourer, which is purchased. The labourer remains formally free.

To what extent does this classical productive rationality still prevail, and is it likely to continue to be dominant?

Early capitalism operated with relatively small productive units, and with a more or less intuitively intelligible, fairly simple technology. Neither of these conditions applies now. In the days when they did apply, they made 'rationality by natural selection' plausible. It was not supposed that individuals were necessarily wise and rational in their strategic choices: but the coexistence of many such competing individuals helped ensure that those who were indeed wise prevailed, and survived, and thus efficiency was enhanced.

The very large and often state-linked technical innovations, requiring an enormous infrastructure, so characteristic of later and advanced economies, no longer lend themselves quite so easily to this model. The commitment of resources is so great as frequently to be irreversible. Hence the continuation of a given socio-technical option may be preferable to its reversal. It may be maintained even if, in the light of searching scrutiny, it is not optimal. The complex interdependence of an advanced modern economy may in any case make global cost-effectiveness evaluations of this kind very difficult. Ironically, in virtue of the extreme 'functional interdependence' of its parts, a very highly developed society recalls some of those very features of a traditional society which had, it is said, prevented it from developing a rational economy. The interconnections between diverse aspects and areas is so great that excessively unscrupulous pursuit of efficiency at any one point may well have intolerable effects on other parts of the system. Perhaps one should not exaggerate this; and at the level of detail, innovation does no doubt continue unabated. But major and global innovation may well, once again, have acquired or recovered what one may call a political rather than economic logic: single-shot irreversible decisions, influenced by complex and incommensurate considerations, may be becoming more important than decisions which can be accurately and quantitatively assessed in the light of clear criteria.

In one sphere, the diminution of classical rationality is unmistakable. The ruthless deployment of human labour power, governed by considerations of efficiency alone, is largely a matter of the past, at any rate in the more developed and affluent societies. People could only be subjected to that kind of rationality if they were first weakened by indigence, and if their formal freedom, as the Left always liked to point out, was combined with economic powerlessness and dependence. In developed countries, it is by now notorious that the local labour force cannot be impelled either to move geographically in pursuit of work, or to accept ill-paid or otherwise unattractive employment, even when jobs are scarce. For economic activities which require such low-grade, malleable, 'rationally' usable labour, developed countries rely on migrants and *Gastarbeiter* from more impoverished lands. Welfare provisions, a general affluence, a high level of expectation, home ownership and other forms of economic and social rootedness all cushion and protect the working class from the old ruthless exploitative rationality.

It is interesting to note that these privileges of affluence, the liberation from economic vulnerability and subjection, seem to shield men from both rational and irrational, from both capitalist and traditionalist types of subjection. In a society in which the rich have in effect exhausted all material forms of pleasure and comfort, but where the competition for status is fierce, and where unemployment is also rife, one would logically expect a dramatic expansion of domestic service. The old conspicuous use of retainers for the enhancement of status might be expected to return, with a vengeance. In fact, however, the lower orders in affluent societies do not generally allow themselves to be impelled to a servile status, even during periods of prolonged mass unemployment. Domestic servants are relatively rare and expensive.

Contrary to the expectations of many economists and of some sociologists, the new impediments to ruthless economic instrumental efficiency not only do not seem to be harmful, but may be positively beneficial, even by purely economic criteria. Japanese industrial attitudes are notoriously 'feudal'. Companies provide lifelong security for their employees, comparable to the kind of safety which the peasant enjoyed when his relation to his overlord was simultaneously economic, social, and political: loyalty is traded for simultaneously economic and political insurance. There is also a notorious stability of status and, to a Western sensibility, an exaggerated respect for seniority. Given such an ethos, any student of classical economics and sociology would naturally conclude that the Japanese economy must be sluggish. It cannot conceivably compete with socially more liberal, mobile, ruthless, and individualist societies, unrestrained by tradition, loyalty, and deference. As we all know, this most plausible expectation has been dramatically falsified. The most distinguished sociologist of modern Japan has gone on to speculate whether Japan rather than the West is the model of the dominant future form of industrial society.[1] Developments in other parts of Southeast Asia suggest that the current late stage of the industrial revolution favours Confucian rather than Calvinistic societies.

So social sensitivity, and the imposition of limits on the

[1] R. Dore, *British Factory, Japanese Factory* (Allen and Unwin, London, 1973).

authority of merely economic considerations, seem in favourable circumstances to be economically advantageous, rather than detrimental. The same is not true of the imposition of predominantly political constraints. If there is a single reason for the generally poor economic performance of 'socialist' societies, it is to be found in the fact that managers occupy positions in the single national economic-political-ideological hierarchy. They are compelled to be preoccupied with political intrigue *within it*, and have little time or inclination, or even the equipment and information, to attend to economic performance. This phenomenon may also be duplicated in part in large corporations and bureaucracies in the non-socialist world.

Economy Two: consumption

In the field of production, the situation may be ambiguous; in consumption, there may be less room for doubt about the general trend. Early industrialism may have been characterized, in contrast to the social order which preceded it, by sobriety, restraint, thrift, method, and a tendency to plough back profits, rather than dissipating them in pleasure, power, and display. If the Puritans were sober at work, they were even more sober at leisure. In fact it is reasonable to suspect that their work sobriety only saw the light of day because rationality pervaded their entire souls. Rationality in *production* only emerged because there were men addicted to rationality in their total life-style; it was not engendered by the internal logic of the work situation. Later developers could be rational at work, because it was now seen to pay, without being wedded to a rational style in all aspects of life, but the earlier ones were rational at work only because rationality was integral to their lives. But what happens under later industrialism?

A certain measure of orderliness may still be observed. For one thing, pervasive affluence hinges on mass production and mass consumption. Wealth is so to speak modular. The elements of consumption are composed of units that are standardized, so that in the main the individual consumer is only given the choice concerning just how he combines prefabricated items. The constituent elements of his life-style he must share with his fellows. He has to buy them in what is in effect the same global supermarket: only the selection from a standard range of choices can be his own.

At the same time, the health of the economy requires, for well-known Keynesian reasons, a widespread consumption orientation, which is indeed very pervasive and deeply rooted. In what sense, if at all, can it be called rational? Some have claimed that *pre*-agrarian man showed good sense and genuine rationality, by being very restrained in his needs and demands.[1] By contrast, agrarian man was doomed, by well-known Malthusian mechanisms, to live under the shadow of starvation. The need for labour-power and for defence-power impelled agrarian society to value offspring, or at any rate male offspring. But the resources available to a society based on agriculture, yet devoid of an expanding technology, were such as to ensure that a major part of the population was never very far removed from hunger. Hence the entire society was liable to suffer during any setbacks in agricultural production, whether occasioned by natural disasters or social disruption. The situation could be aggravated during the early stages of the transition to industrialism.

All this heritage left early industrial man with a set of clearly delineated, relatively 'objective' values – a sufficiency of nourishment, shelter, security, freedom from continuous and totally exhausting work, access to the available medical care, a reasonable expectation of living out the full human span, and finally access through education to the new, literate, citizenship-conferring culture. There is of course no iron law of logic obliging a man to want these things; but it is natural that he should do so, if he retains the vivid recollection of the hunger and pain of agrarian society, and of the social conditions accompanying the transition from it, and the clear perception that these things need no longer be borne. It is now manifest that they can be avoided with the

[1] M. Sahlins, *Stone Age Economics* (Tavistock, London, 1974).

technology at our disposal. The resources available to developed society seem capable of satisfying these aims, without excessive difficulty. What else could the heart desire?

As far as the biological constitution of human beings is concerned, the answer would seem to be – *very little*. Wealth over and above this minimum can, on the whole, only be used for the enhancement of a person's social position in relation to his fellows. It can only be deployed in the pursuit of status and prestige. But what gives the ownership of objects such a power? In some measure, the recollection of drudgery or even hunger may still be sufficiently powerful, and affluence still far from complete: this endows some of the material status symbols with a genuine 'objective' attractiveness. But in developed societies, the time when this will cease to be true must now be fairly close. The exact choice of the material symbols deployed then constitutes a kind of cultural accident; it all depends on what a given culture happens to use so as to render ranking visible, to grant a man the satisfaction of elevating him above his fellows. The counter-productive and self-contradictory aspects of continued symbolic valuation of otherwise useless material wealth have been widely noted. Cars, once genuinely useful, have but a limited value in a town whose streets are blocked by traffic, and where parking is virtually impossible.

The imperatives governing production may continue to impose a certain discipline and order on those who are involved in it, during the periods when they are indeed so employed. But the amount of time spent in work is diminishing. What of the impact of that rapidly increasing proportion of time, and of personnel, no longer engaged in work? The patterns of consumption are no longer such as to encourage orderly attention, sobriety, and cool thought, or any of the other famous attributes of the old rationality. On the contrary: the diverse gadgets or packages which are supplied to the public are designed to be easy-on-the-mind, to be as smooth and intuitively accessible as possible. The industrially constructed environment consists of servo-artefacts of different kinds, whose controls are as user-friendly, as effortless, as intuitively obvious, as the designer's ingenuity can make them. This kind of environment encourages a relaxed ease, rather than tight order and discipline. Affluent man is liable to see the world as an extension of such an easily manipulated and seemingly self-explanatory environment. Notoriously, he is attracted by facile metaphysics, which present him with a similarly user-friendly universe, easily accessible to cognitive penetration. It is at any rate conceivable that the society which is in full possession of the benefits of rational production will also indulge the wildest excesses of unreason in its culture.[1]

Cognition

Cognition is the sphere in which the victory of the rationalist style or conception is least open to genuine doubt. The form of knowledge which receives serious respect in developed society – science – is governed by a set of rules which continues to have much affinity with those which Descartes had proposed for the rational comportment of the human mind. His Table of Commandments still dominates. 'Custom and example' are not allowed any but a temporary and presumptive authority; it is the custom and example of a fairly select and trained scientific community, not of the common run of men; yet there are no privileged knowers, no organization is allowed to claim cognitive monopoly, there are no privileged events or objects. Logical cogency and evidence are king. Explanations are required to be symmetrical, and they are subject to tests not under the control of the system of ideas that is under scrutiny. Belief systems are not allowed to set up closed circuits, in which a sacred and privileged background picture leads privileged validators to perceive and recognize sacred evidence, which then re-confirms the initial Picture. So the brazen circularity of agrarian thought, where the very rules of inquiry ensure the confirmation of the initial world-picture and are its corollary, is proscribed. A vision of the

---

[1] D. Bell, *The Cultural Contradictions of Capitalism* (Heinemann, London, 1976). Bell holds all this to constitute a kind of contradiction. To me, it seems to have a kind of natural fit and logic.

world is not allowed to dictate rules of evidence, with privileged sources, which then confirm the vision itself. One clear and distinct and self-justifying idea dominates: namely, that anything which is in conflict with independently, symmetrically established evidence, cannot be true.

The sovereignty of evidence is really the crucial survivor from amongst those luminous self-vindicating ideas, which Descartes hoped to use in the cognitive reconstruction of his world. The *modus tolens*, the elimination of ideas contradicted by fact, is the one offer which the rational mind cannot refuse. So truth comes under the control of nature, i.e. a unified system external to society and independent of it, and it is not subject to any social requirements. Nature and society are distinct, as are church and state. The separation of all separable issues is a respected part of the dominant ethic of cognitive comportment. The kind of cognitive bulk-purchase or package-dealing which in the past protected beliefs from effective scrutiny is proscribed.

Irrationalist trends indisputably do exist, and may be prominent in the wider society, but they are not conspicuous *within* the actual practice of science. Oddly enough, they actually proliferate in the meta-theory of science, and also within fringe subjects of questionable scientific status. Theories concerning science frequently stress its irrationality in a number of ways. Some claim that, contrary to its own self-image, its direction is not rationally determined, but is guided by some obscure social mechanism or intuitive process.

Moreover, its basic and guiding ideas cannot be justified, as Descartes had hoped they could be: they are themselves the fruit of an unjustified and hence arbitrary commitment, a *leap*, as the erstwhile fashionable phrase would have it. This is the widely used *tu quoque* argument of irrationalism: reason herself is as arbitrary as anything else; hence, the argument goes on, we are fully justified in any arbitrary claim we care to make. We are all of us equal, rationalists and others, in our inescapable unreason. All visions are irrational, and none are less so than others.[1]

---

[1] W.W. Bartley III, *The Retreat to Commitment* (2nd edn, La Salle, London, 1984).

These arguments contain grains of a wildly exaggerated truth. They ignore the fact that the internal rational organization of science, the symmetry and orderliness, and the systematic submission to testing of theories by data *not* under the control of their own interpretation, do most profoundly and radically distinguish it from other belief systems. The merit of this unique style is pragmatically vindicated by the dramatic, and often literally devastating, superiority of the technology based on it.

Culture

The overall way in which men feel and think has never been fully dominated by the rationalist ideal. Culture has seldom been properly subjected either to orderly systematization, or to instrumental efficacy. Undoubtedly things have moved in this direction in some measure during the emergence of modern industrial life. Economic life had done so, at the same time as it became more separate from social and political life. Yet economic life could only do so because the social style had itself moved in that direction. Within social life itself, a certain measure of rationalization was noticable. This was no doubt a precondition of the corresponding change in the economy. The equalization, or at least the systematization, of statuses, the standardization of measures and procedures and of the law, of communication systems, were all part and parcel of the cultural infrastructure. (Max Weber, the great observer of rationality as a precondition of industrialism, faced a little difficulty in the fact that the country in which rational production first emerged was also one committed to a messy, untidy Common Law, and resisted Roman Law.) A greater orderliness in domestic relations, a greater tendency to punctuality, a diffusion of literacy, and a pervasive bureaucratization, orderly recruitment of personnel, and allocation and definition of function, were all part and parcel of it.

But for a variety of well-known reasons, personal relations and culture are not as amenable as production or cognition to a full systematization and a cost-benefit evaluation by clear criteria.

The process did not and simply could not go nearly as far in this field as it did in the others. It is virtually impossible to specify clear and exclusive criteria for satisfactory basic personal relationships. Even if the sway of complex, stable, multi-strand relationships, which had once dominated the economy and the traditional world, was now markedly reduced, the residue which survived became all the more important: in the choice of a spouse or a piece of prose, no clear and distinct criterion or principle can easily be invoked. A man who absorbs a culture and its values resembles a person learning a language or a dance, rather than a person pursuing a clearly specified and exclusive aim. He is not a maximizer or a rule-applier. He can learn to avoid gaffes, but there is often no way of defining precisely that which should count as a gaffe. Sometimes one can learn to guess what would constitute a gaffe in the culture, simply by having a kind of *feel* of its general style; but it is not always so. Some cultural proscriptions are liable to be almost deliberately idiosyncratic, and nothing other than familiarity with the tabu in question can help one behave acceptably.

This is indeed the way in which cultures impose their authority: strangers tread at their own peril. They betray the fact that they are not proper members by their lack of familiarity with rules which they *cannot* work out for themselves. These have no rhyme or reason. Cartesian rules cannot help you to become acceptable in a coterie or a culture. Unreason is an essential part of social control, of group definition and status ascription. In a rational world, such traps for the unwary would not exist: reason has no favourites, and is available to all. But in social worlds as we know them, in cultures, unreason is an important gatekeeper. Even the irregularity of some verbs may have its role to play in the social deployment of speech and the maintenance of social order. Grammar may, like military discipline or etiquette or protocol, actually *need* its arbitrarinesses. He who has not mastered the exceptions betrays his outsider status. Irregular verbs make their contribution to social discipline. It is good, from a social viewpoint, that some people should feel insecure all of the time, and that all should feel insecure some of the time. It keeps them on their toes, and helps maintain respect for the established order.

Weber, the great sociologist of rationality, was a little ambivalent about the relationship of rationality to high culture. In part he supposed that an obsessive rationality entered even into the arts, and also affected the attitude of the puritans to art – i.e. his favoured carriers of the rational spirit. By depriving religion of its reliance on audio-visual aids, they strengthened the Inner Voice and made their invaluable contribution to a rule-abiding society, to that *innere Führung* which became the Kantian slogan of the post-war *Bundeswehr*. But art and patronage go together, and neither has any place in a world respecting principles. Max Weber also noted that the Puritans had enough sensitivity and greatness of heart to suspend their rationalism when faced with truly great art.[1]

Not only has the sphere of culture remained more immune than some others to the spread of rationality; latter-day irrationalist or non-rationalist counter-currents have been specially strong within it. This has already been noted in connection with patterns of consumption. In a way, the irrationalization of culture is the obverse of the pervasive rationalization of cognition. It is precisely because serious, cumulative, powerful cognitive inquiry has been hived off from the rest of our conceptual life that this residue is liable to be thrown back onto its own resources, which had previously operated more pervasively. 'Culture', in the non-anthropological narrower sense the term has now acquired in developed societies, is a kind of buttermilk – the symbolic activities left over as a residue when serious cognition (science) and production have been abstracted.

Humanity has inherited, from the age of the late and highly developed agrarian literate civilizations, the expectation or hope that the fundamental features of the social order can be vindicated by *proof*. The clerics of those civilizations had shifted

---

[1] Max Weber, *The Protestant Ethic and the Spirit of Capitalism* (Unwin University Books, London, 1930; repr. 1965), p. 168ff.

the centre of gravity of social validation from the poetic-naive vindication-by-story of the Heroic Age to the later scholastic predilection for legitimation-by-proof. That was their speciality, which distinguished them from their rivals, the freelance ecstatic shamans. Given a stable cognitive capital or base, sacred, endowed with so to speak constitutionally entrenched premisses, the clerics could provide a firm foundation, in a style which underscored the authority of the literates as against the ecstatics. These doctrinal bases then rigorously fortified the social order, at any rate to the satisfaction of the clerics in question.

The society which replaced these civilizations, whose economic and political foundation is, precisely, cognitive and productive growth, and which also brings instability in its train, cannot really use its genuine cognitive accomplishments for the purposes of social legitimation, though some of its intellectuals have striven to do so. Its cognitive bank of ideas is open: consensus is not imposed, innovation and experimentation are permitted and encouraged and required, no element within it is profoundly entrenched, or protected by sacredness from query or modification. Change itself is legitimate, expected and valued. This being so, to use genuinely cognitive convictions as bases for the social order is to build on sand. Precisely because they make a genuine contribution to serious cognition, they are precluded from providing hallowed, firm, suitable bases for a social order. They are ephemeral, and are meant to be such. So the sphere of *legitimative* thought comes to be separated, not completely perhaps, but to a very considerable extent, from the sphere of genuine knowledge.

The separation is indeed far from complete. The belief systems inherited from the cognitively stable and authoritarian agrarian civilizations, and deployed in social symbolism, are retained, but in a muted style. The extent to which they are credited with genuine cognitive content is ambiguous, and subject to a kind of sliding-scale adjustment, varying with context, personal intuition, and the success or failure of the cognitive claim in question. At the same time, new secular ideologies are often erected around putative truths of science and/or history. However, the most ambitious and politically successful of these had, by 1990, suffered a dramatic collapse.

Power and politics

In many of its procedural ways, politics is pervasively rationalized. The state and political parties are both heavily bureaucratized. Consent has its routines. The language of ordinary political debate is predominantly utilitarian. But when major and imponderable issues are faced, politics does of course suffer from the loss of that absolute and confident validation which is the inescapable fate of societies corroded by the rationalist spirit. Consequently there is a tendency to oscillate between a rationalistic-bureaucratic style and another one, which Max Weber, in a phrase destined to enter and pervade popular use, called 'charismatic': a dramatic, unreasoning, total claim to authority, made in an irrationalist or anti-rational spirit, brazenly spurning even the appearance of logical support. The two principles can fuse at the top: Napoleon provided the very paradigm of charisma, yet also gave his name to the model of an orderly legal code and tidy administrative system.

The appeal of charisma may be rationalized at a more abstract and general level by the claim that the sources of human vitality, and hence also of all ultimate authority, are not to be found in reason, but in 'blood' or passion or commitment. A view of this kind was of course a central theme of Fascist and Nazi ideology.

Politics is less rationalizable than the economy, and very much less so than cognition. Ordinary day-to-day politics may indeed be a matter of bargaining about the division of spoils, and, as such, not very different from economic negotiation. But at the same time politics is about power, coercion, ultimate authority. This may not be evident in peaceful or consensual times, when authority is uncontested. But when serious and total conflicts do occur, whether they be civil or inter-national, the un-negotiable totality of the conflict becomes manifest. In modern times this is aggravated by the fact that the issue is not merely about who is endowed with power, but is also very often concerned with what *kind* of power it is to be. Conflicts occur not merely between individuals or groups competing for the control of a given organizational structure, but between rival ideas concerning the nature of social organization itself. Either way, the conflict is then unlikely to be open to a rational, 'optimizing', negotiated solution.

The partisans of total, charismatic politics do in fact invoke and frequently conflate two quite distinct anti-rationalist arguments. There is first the communalistic argument: life *is* participation in a shared culture and community, not haggling in a market. A genuinely cultural community is a system of many-stranded relationships, of an ongoing dialogue, in which one participates, but which cannot be reduced to the pursuit of any one aim, and within which rational calculation is inappropriate or offensive. A community is not an enterprise, Michael Oakeshott insists.[1] In 'functional' systems of interlocking institutions, any action is bound to have many and complex repercussions on all parts of the system, and so a ruthless 'rationality' would be wholly inappropriate. One must *feel* the right move which is to be made in the dance, rather than seek the most cost-effective strategy.

Second, there is the Dark Gods argument. Human vitality springs from deep, presumably biological roots. The drives which truly activate us find fulfilment in passionate human relationships and in communal participation, preferably ecstatic, and not in the maximization of gain, or indeed of anything else. Thus only, and in no other way, is genuine satisfaction to be found. Reason is irrelevant or positively noxious, either to the definition of aims, or even to the selection of means: a real passion cannot be constrained either to define or seek its object by a finely tuned calculation.

If you add the assumption that the 'organic' community of culture is also a racial or genetic one, the communalistic and the biological anti-rational doctrine will tend to fuse into a single

[1] M. Oakeshott, *On Human Conduct* (Clarendon Press, Oxford, 1975).

doctrine. The communalistic variant of political irrationalism is liable on occasion to underlie, romanticism of the Left as well as that of the Right.

The variety of rational experience

The Impotence of Reason theme had a number of threads. One was the inability, contrary to Descartes's hopes and anticipations, of Reason to justify its own procedures, of *proving* them to be sound. Another was the incapacity of Reason, not merely to demonstrate conclusively, but even to impose her procedures, in fields other than cognition. Kant supposed otherwise: he believed that the very same inner compulsion which impelled men to systematize their ideas, to subsume them under orderly symmetrical rules and strive to unify them, also caused them to feel an obligation to do the same in their moral lives, to treat like cases alike without fear or favour. He did not suppose that men generally lived up to this obligation and actually fulfilled its commands; but he did think (and his system required this) that all men recognized in their hearts, with vigour – even if they did not obey – the need to act as rule-bound, norm-respecting, conscientious puritans. Even the most hardened villain, Kant claimed, regretted in his heart that he was not acting like a puritan.

In all this, Kant was mistaken. Many, many cultures do not instil one ethic of a symmetrical application of rules, but on the contrary an ethic of asymmetrical loyalty. But it is interesting to ask why the orderliness-compulsion, the implementation of Cartesian-Kantian rationality, does all in all prevail in modern cognition, though not elsewhere.

In cognition, though it is incapable of proving that it *must* work and is reliable, in fact it unquestionably does work, and has been vindicated pragmatically. The astonishing and unquestionable power of the technology born of rational inquiry is such that the majority of mankind – and in particular those men eager to increase their wealth and/or power – are eager to emulate it. Its devotees may combine it with all kinds of irrationality, but for all that they do deeply respect it. They consult the engineer as well as the astrologer, even if they do also consult the latter. But no similar pragmatic vindication endorses compulsive orderliness in the moral sphere. Moral orderliness may have initially engendered cognition and economic rationality, but once these have proved their power, they are emulated on their own.

It may well be that the early rational producers had to have their souls pervaded by a compulsive rationality before they could (without, initially, any rational hope of benefiting thereby) also become committed to rational production; but, as Max Weber noted, once the wealth-producing potential of the new productive style became manifest, many others could and did adopt it, without any longer being impelled to it by the devious, not to say bizarre, motivation which Weber attributed to the puritan progenitors of modern rationality.

So it is no use trying to impose a rationalistic, universalistic, egalitarian ethic on mankind with the argument that the productive style which is the condition of the life-style to which you are eager to become accustomed *also* obliges you to behave in a certain way. It is perfectly obvious by now that one can accept elements of that rationality, notably its implementation in the exploration of nature and in production, without for all that in any way also accepting it in other spheres. This may be regrettable, but it seems to be so. Pragmatic considerations underwrite Reason in cognition; they underwrite and condition it in production during the early period of expansion, but they do so only selectively during later stages; and they do not seem to underwrite it in morals at all, or only in a most debatable and contestable manner.

The uneven distribution of rationality is also interesting in other contexts. It was probably essential to the development of the modern world as we know it that rational production, capitalism, preceded really powerful technology, but also that this powerful technology appeared on the scene not too long after the victory of capitalism in the first Industrial Revolution. Had really powerful technology been available earlier, its military and political potential would have been manifest, and it would have been seized by the modern absolutist state, which in turn would presumably have led to the throttling of the emergence of pluralist and democratic politics in the nineteenth century. If, on the other hand, the new technology had not arrived on the scene fairly soon after the Industrial Revolution, and made possible the continuous expansion of production and hence the raising of living standards which took place, it is probable that the pessimistic predictions of the early classical economists and, following them, of Marx, would have been fulfilled, and rational production would have ground to a halt, like so many earlier 'proto-industrializations'.[1] Rational production and commercialization, unaccompanied by a major scientific and technological revolution, can raise living standards, but before too long runs up against the Principle of Diminishing Returns, and does not have that world-transforming potential which a joint productive *and* cognitive rationalization did have.

As for the future – it is of course perfectly conceivable that rationality will once again withdraw to a ghetto, to a small productive and cognitive zone, and that other aspects of life and thought will be governed by quite different principles.

---

[1] cf. E.A. Wrigley, *People, Cities and Wealth: The transformation of traditional society* (Blackwell, Oxford, 1987).

8
Prometheus Perplexed

Autonomy lost

One of the central themes, perhaps indeed the central obsession, of Cartesian rationalism is the aspiration for autonomy. There is the overwhelming desire for a kind of self-creation, for bringing forth a self and a world not simply taken over from an unexamined, accidental, contingent inheritance. Rationalism is the philosophy of the New Broom. Man makes himself, and he does so *rationally*. Cultural accumulation is irrational: it is a blind process. If our thought and valuation are its fruits, they are unworthy of our trust in our identification.

Descartes's ego wishes to be unbeholden both to the past *and* to any underlying and unexamined infrastructure: it must operate with its own tools, self-made, transparent, and self-guaranteeing. Man uses Reason to make himself. The tools are not borrowed or taken over; they are made with the same rigorous scrutiny which is also to be applied to the output which they are to produce. In the pursuit of cogent reasons, which is a corollary of this aspiration, the requirement of rational guarantee carries with it the need for autonomy. What you have not made and tested yourself, you cannot trust. The unexamined inheritance of mere *custom and example*, of the jetsam of history, of the bank of custom of a culture, can never satisfy the stringent rationalist criteria. Autonomy requires reason, and reason requires autonomy.

To what extent can this Promethean aspiration to autarchy and self-creation be satisfied? The answer is simple. *It cannot.* We cannot, as Descartes in effect planned and desired, excogitate ourselves *ex nihilo*. We cannot think up, from the recesses of our private consciousness, both the criteria *and* the tools required for the erection of a new conceptual and cognitive edifice, destined no longer to be beholden to any prior history. Such an aspiration towards such a 'cosmic exile' is pervasive in the history of modern Western thought. It has been derided by many, including Karl Marx:

> The...doctrine that men are products of circumstances forgets that circumstances are changed...by men and that the educator went himself to be educated. Hence this doctrine necessarily arrives at dividing society into two parts, of which one towers above society...[1]

Marx was one of the many Providentialists: he could deride the aspiration to stand outside society and to tell it where to go. He could do so because he believed, benighted Hegelian that he was, that he had access to knowledge concerning where it *must* go. We could trust the World-Process, and so we neither need nor can stand outside it so as to assess it. No towering above the social process is required: we can trust 'revolutionizing practice', his version of the Holy Ghost. He knew that practice was bound to take us to a good place. He analysed the forces which propelled the world in a given direction, and was content to trust and endorse the wisdom of that direction. The excellence of the destination in turn would be validated by the fact that this was where the world was indeed going.

By prejudging the issue of the nature of the world, you could give yourself dispensation from the unsatisfiable Cartesian obligation to scrutinize independently our way of knowing that world. The acceptance of our cognitive equipment or custom came with the prior acceptance of the world as a whole, and knowledge (of that self-same world) was an integral part of that

---

[1] Karl Marx, *Theses on Feuerbach*.

accepted world. Because you think you know what the world is like, and what (beneficent) place knowledge plays within it, you can trust that knowledge and refrain from a radical scrutiny of it. A *general* complacency implies a specific one concerning our cognitive practices. In a different tradition and idiom, Quine in our time teaches much the same: all's well with the world and above all our cognitive habits, and cosmic exile is not mandatory.

It may be easy to see why the Promethean aspiration to exile is absurd; but it is more important still to see why it is both inescapable and mandatory. This aspiration *defines* us, even though it cannot be fulfilled. We are what we are, precisely because this strange aspiration is so deeply inherent in our thought. We may never fulfil its demands fully, but we are what we are because our intellectual ancestors tried so hard, and the effort has entered our souls and pervaded our cognitive custom. We are a race of failed Prometheuses. Rationalism is our destiny. It is not our option, and still less our disease. We are not free of culture, of Custom and Example: but it is of the essence of *our* culture that it is rooted in the rationalist aspirations.

Yet it is true that we were bound to fail. It is impossible to deny that the aspiration, essential though it may be to our identity, and our civilization, is also absurd. We cannot engender the tools which in turn would make the tools with which we would then think, in order to render ourselves truly independent of all earlier toolmakers and to create our world without the help of prejudice. We rightly distrust those who accepted and trusted their own cultures. Spinoza was acutely aware of the problem.

> ...in order to work iron, a hammer is needed, and the hammer cannot be forthcoming unless it has been made but, in order to make it, there was need of another hammer...and so on to infinity.[1]

If total autonomy through spontaneous conceptual generation is impossible, what remains? What was the valid kernel in this, the

---

[1] B. Spinoza, *De Intellectus Emendatione*, in *Ethics and De Intellectus Emendatione* (London, 1910; first published 1677).

deepest of all rationalist aspirations? What was the situation which this aspiration reflected?

If the total autonomy of self-generation is an illusion, which it is, what *does* remain is the profound *coupure* between a new and pervasively rational society, and the old, predominantly traditional one.

The Providentialists try to provide an alternative to Cosmic Exile by the doctrine that Reason was the heir to an old and dominant current, pervading all history or even all life. A Manifest Destiny led from the amoeba or Early Man to Newton and Einstein. This is not so: Reason is a foundling, and not an heir of an old line, and its identity or justification, such as it is, is forged without the benefit of ancient lineage. A bastard of nature cannot be vindicated by ancestry but only, at best, by achievement. The Siege Mentality, not Pre-established Harmony, is the right spirit in the philosophy of Reason.

The Cosmic Exile, the opting out of culture, is impracticable. But it constitutes the noble and wholly appropriate charter or myth of a new kind of culture, a new system of a distinctively *Cartesian* kind of Custom and Example. Custom was not transcended: *but a new kind of custom altogether was initiated*. The separation of referential cognition from other activities, the systematic submission of cognitive claim to a severely extra-social centralized court of appeal (under the slogan of 'clear and distinct ideas', or of 'experience'), and the establishment of a single currency of reference, had burst open the limits of knowledge. It initiated and made possible an age of totally unprecedented, fabulous cognitive and economic growth. Through its associated technology, it brought the Malthusian age to an end. Henceforth resources would, and generally did, grow faster than population. Coercive political systems were no longer imposed on mankind by the need to enforce an inevitably unjust distribution on members of society endowed with inherently limited resources. Oppression, from now on, was to be our option, but no longer our destiny.

All this, once and for good, totally separated and distinguished this Sorcerer's Apprentice society from all predecessors. But at the same time, it also deprived it of the supports and solaces hitherto available to mankind. You cannot have it both ways; you cannot have both knowledge and illusion. Or rather: you cannot *consistently* have them both. Mankind may yet learn to be systematically inconsistent. Strenuous efforts are under way to achieve just this. But that is another story.

Descartes was misguided in supposing that he could go it alone. But a *collectivity* of cognitive individualists can achieve something fundamental, even if it is not exactly what Descartes anticipated. Likewise, Descartes was wrong in supposing that he could liberate himself from culture, from custom and example. The truth of the matter is that what was emerging was a radically different new kind of culture, a new custom which he helped codify.

But it was not simply one further culture amongst others. It was new in kind, and was built on wholly new principles. All the same, it was *a* culture, rather than a transcendence of all culture, as Descartes had supposed. It had its own and distinctive compulsions, and they too had their social roots, as Weber taught. A new kind of society had engendered a new species of compulsion, and it was in turn sustained by them. The significance of Max Weber as *the* sociologist of rationality is that he gives us a theory of how this very distinctive kind of culture, one making the scientific understanding of nature and its technological domination possible, could come about. From the viewpoint of sociology, the significance of the great rationalist philosophers is that, under the guise of an account of the human mind as such, they give us a portrait, from the inside, of the unique new kind of Custom and Example.

The practice of scrutiny-by-doubt, which Descartes proposed as a means of conceptual purification, is in fact an excellent customs procedure for vetting what could, and what could not, be granted an entry point into the new culture. The precise nature of that clarity and distinctness, which was to be applied by the cognitive Customs and Excise men, came to be much better understood by the empiricists who followed Descartes, though he did to some extent have the right general idea. The logical compulsion which owes nothing to culture, and which can consequently give us a vision of nature valid for all cultures and rooted in none, is in the end quite simple: the givenness of *data* (present in Descartes's thought as the immediate availability of the thinking substance to itself), plus the simple logical principle that no generalization incompatible with given data may be accepted.

So the heroic erection of an entire world by a single individual, the Crusoe style of cognition, the use of naught but our own self-tested and self-produced resources, is indeed impossible. But the almost-as-heroic establishment of a new kind of culture, endowed with a new kind of epistemic constitution, *was* possible, and it did take place. We were bound to fail, but we were also bound to try; and the effort bore magnificent fruit, even if it was not all that the Founder Rationalist had proposed. The abortive effort defined a new civilization. The new rationality had a history, and had tremendous consequences: historical sociology has tried to grapple with both, and Max Weber's work, whether right or wrong in details, remains valid as the outstanding formulation of the problem.

How did we build this new world? It was built up by new men imbued by the Crusoe/Descartes spirit. Robinson Crusoe was a man who carried the essential part of his culture in himself and could re-erect it on the island on his own. He needed no complementary fellow-specialists, whose zone of competence he is ritually or legally barred from entering. In other words, all the specialisms of his culture employ the same idiom, which he has mastered, and they are open to him.

That which was presented as a solitary, Descartes-Crusoe enterprise, was in fact the charter of a radically new social order. But to say this is *not* to reduce the philosophical content of individualist rationalism to its social role. This is not a sociologically reductionist position. The philosophical *content* genuinely illuminates the manner in which the new social order works: it really is individualist, and it is based on genuine and cumulative knowledge. The philosophy and the sociology of rationality cannot be brought together. Neither is reduced to the other.

The rationalists did not, as Descartes thought, transcend culture. They created and codified a distinctive, special, individualist culture, one distinguished from its predecessors by incomparably greater cognitive power – and by importance in the sphere of moral legitimation. Mankind had passed through three stages – the age of ritual, the age of spurious proof, and the age of absence of proof. They charted the rules of this third condition.

Transcendence and relativism

A conspicuous feature of Rationalism was its aspiration for cognitive self-creation: the rationalist desires to be a totally *self-made-man*, unsullied by the network of shady and unsecured cognitive debt, by the accidental and compromise-sullied accommodations which make up the earlier intellectual history of mankind. It had been such unprincipled opportunism and compromise that had inhibited genuine intellectual growth. It is not only pride or puritanism which impel the rationalist in this direction: it is also the reflection that principles of operation which he has not himself established, he is not entitled to underwrite. They are unsafe, and it would be irresponsible to do so. He cannot really be sure about the cognitive quality and reliability of what they produce. It is not an *appellation contrôlée* growth. He really cannot, in all conscience, authenticate their produce. He cannot make himself accountable for their claims.

The second, closely related and equally important, trait is the pursuit of *transcendence*. Rationalism unquestionably conceives knowledge as the attainment *of* something external and independent: it must not be merely something which is, so to speak, internally spawned by the organism. This would seem to constitute a contradiction: the rationalist wants to produce knowledge from his own resources, and he also wants it to refer to something objective.

There is no contradiction. In fact, autonomy and transcendence are very closely linked: it is *just* because knowledge is independent that it displays the autonomy of its possessor. Conversely, only the autonomous inquirer can claim genuine and transcendent knowledge. The unfree inquirer, if he attains truth at all, can only do so by grace of his master, by kind permission of the agency, natural or cultural, which happens to manipulate him. Such knowledge, conditional on the whim of an overlord, is worthless.

So there is a kind of paradox: the citizen of a rational order claims autonomy precisely because the contents of his knowledge, the cognitive claims he makes, are totally independent of him. He did not *make it up*; he *found* it. You might have expected the opposite. You might have expected the autonomous agent to *create* his object. Not so. But the paradox is only apparent.

Referential claims made in the rational spirit are, first of all, separated from all other functions or aspirations. They do not at the same time, for instance, perform some internal services for the morale or cohesion or discipline of the organism within which they occur. (In this sense, they are very much part of a society which practises the Division of Labour, and consequently can, in each sphere, apply a single and lucid criterion, and pass objective judgement.) Convictions are subject to one criterion only, namely referential and explanatory power. They observe the rules of what may be called Cartesian/empiricist method: separation of all questions and issues, and the subjection of all claims to tests not under their own control. This, in conjunction with the strong impulsion to generality and order, seems to have engendered a form of knowledge of astonishing power, and one *not* linked to any one cultural system. It appears that if the world is to be knowable at all, it will yield to this strategy alone. That it is knowable at all, that it does surrender its secrets to such a strategy, if to no other, is a miracle. The question concerning why it should be such a world cannot be answered by the deployment of that strategy itself. As there is no other method, it must remain a secret for us.

We have found that the absurd and unfeasible Robinsonian endeavour to form a world on one's own is but a parable for the perfectly feasible endeavour to set up a rational culture. (At least, we know it is feasible because it has happened. I for one would never have believed it to be possible in advance.) It is not made by a solitary individual, but it obliges all individuals within that culture to behave in a symmetrical way, at least when cognitively well-behaved and whilst taking part in serious inquiry: to claim no special status, and to recognize that the claims of this culture are open to inspection and critique by any one member.

Is this view just one further case of naive self-congratulation? This is not the first time that a society has believed itself to be in possession of a superior, exclusive, and saving truth, and damned all others as benighted heathen. Is this kind of scientism or positivism simply one further piece of ethnocentric complacency, similar to the dogmatism of past beneficiaries of a self-ascribed, supposedly unique and final Revelation? Our romantics, fond of the *tu quoque* argument, would have us think so. They dislike the coldness, power, and the so to speak culturally disembodied character of science, and like to see it downgraded, removed from its pedestal.

If indeed it were one further case of deluded self-glorification, it would be naive vainglory of a rather unusual kind. Science has conquered the world without encountering much resistance, and virtually no *effective* resistance. It is true that it is subject to a great deal of abuse and denigration, both in its home areas and in the regions it has colonized; but for practical purposes, and in the pursuit of the serious business of life (production, coercion), few spurn its help. Most men and societies are eager, often indecently eager, to avail themselves of it. It makes surprisingly few claims for itself nowadays, but then, it does not need to do so: practice speaks louder than words.

The paradox of the present position is that a *pragmatic* argument is offered in support of the *absolutist* pretensions of science, and of the rationalist spirit linked to it. This is indeed so. It only remains to be said that this is no *generalized* pragmatism. It is not claimed that pragmatic criteria, and they alone, should be applied to all choices. What is said is something far more narrow and specific: in the one great and irreversible transition or *coupure* between the traditional and the rational spirit, pragmatic considerations overwhelmingly, and decisively favour one of the two contestants. At one particular crossroads, the verdict of history is categorical, unambiguous, decisive, and irreversible.

Rationalism and empiricism in partnership

For professional philosophers, rationalism is primarily one of the two contestants in the celebrated confrontation with empiricism. We now return to this debate. It is relevant for the present argument, which has reached the point of claiming *transcendence* to be an essential ingredient of the rationalist position and achievement.

What are the mechanics by which that transcendence is achieved? How has this transcendence been achieved?

The paradox is that it is precisely *empiricism* which achieved the aim of rationalism (namely transcendence); and it is *rationalism* which achieved the aim of empiricism (sensitivity to the external world). The two seeming opponents were in fact complementary. Neither could function without the other. Each, strangely enough, performed the task of the other.

It is useful to refine the notion of transcendence. In early rationalism, a double transcendence was involved: transcendence of nature and the senses on the one hand, and independence from the accumulation of social ideas, of culture, on the other. The aspiration for unprecarious, sound knowledge seemed to require the overcoming both of the unreliable, ephemeral, context-bound nature of sense perception, and of social prejudice alike. Each seemed to provide manifestly unsuitable building bricks for a reliable cognitive edifice. But, as it turned out, these two conceptions of transcendence are in no way similar. On the contrary, they are deeply antithetical.

This idea of knowledge of a realm which is beyond the world of the senses and nature is a snare and a delusion. By what conceivable means could we attain knowledge of such a realm? The old rationalist supposition that the internal cogency, the compulsiveness of our ideas and their interconnection, could somehow propel us into that world, does not survive examination. But, knowledge which on the other hand transcends the bounds, the prejudices and prejudgements of any *one* society and culture is not an illusion but, on the contrary, a glorious and luminous reality. Just how it was achieved remains subject to debate.

What is central to empiricism is the claim that an independent data base, 'experience', sits in judgement over our cognitive claims, but that is *not* under *their* control. Fortunately for mankind, such a data base does indeed appear to be available. Even if never available in pure form, it seems perfectly possible to keep the level of impurity, of 'theory-saturation', down to an acceptably low level. It has indeed been reduced to a level low enough to ensure that 'experience' will perform the task assigned to it: experience, or rather, controlled experimentation, constitutes an effective, socially independent court of appeal for all cognitive claims. Focusing on the data which are in principle available to a single observer, and on their atomization, *has* achieved the transcendence of culturally imposed and dogma-maintaining illusion. Cultural visions work by means of imposing package deals on their clientele. Quine has observed that science faces the world as a corporate body. It would be better to say that pre-scientific beliefs *evade* the world as a corporate body. The empiricist requirement of breaking up what is actually experienced, and turning it into the final court of appeal of theories, does achieve the undermining of the dominance of collective illusion, and replaces it by a cumulative, trans-cultural science. Empiricism is normally seen as a philosophy which insists on the immanence, the this-worldly nature of our knowledge. Its real role has been to achieve *transcendence* of the old culturally imposed limits to our belief.

The contrary view is often heard, but it is simply false. The argument runs as follows: perceptions depend on interpretations, and interpretations are the slaves of social interests. To give a celebrated instance: the working class needs to be liberated from its exploitation by capitalism, and hence needs its morale sustained by a faith in the possibility of socialism, and so it must not be told of the existence of gulags. Sartre openly maintained as much when challenged about his own shameful silence concerning Stalinism: *il faut pas désespérer Billancourt!*

Sartre's argument ran: the bourgeoisie feared socialism, and needed to have its hatred of socialism sustained by a belief in the pervasiveness of gulags under socialism. But on this view gulags as such neither existed nor did not exist. Their 'existence' was a function of the historic position and social interests of the believer.

All this is simply rubbish. Gulags either do or do not exist. Their reality is ascertainable, quite independently of the political opinions of the investigator. Likewise, the Pol Pot regime in Cambodia either did or did not kill an enormous proportion of its own population in an almost unprecedented reign of terror. The fact that it may also suit some Americans to believe that it did so simply is not relevant, contrary to the bizarre moral intuitions of a very distinguished thinker.

Empiricism emerged from the refinement of Cartesian rationalist ideas. The inner compulsions which Descartes wished to use as arbiters of cognitive claims turned out, on more careful examination, to be the data of sense. And by what kind of mechanism did attention to 'experience' achieve this social transcendence? How did it manage to use our sensitivity to make us free of our culture?

Here we reach our second paradox, the fact that it was rationalism which really helped empiricism to perform its task. The empiricist view that we learn from experience is trite: men had always learned from experience, and knew that they did so. This is not exactly a mystery or a new discovery. What made philosophic empiricism important and revolutionary was the implicit addition of the phrase 'men learn by experience *and in no other way*'. And there was also an additional point: conceptual package deals, complex visions, are a way of avoiding the *real* lesson of experience. So experience must be viewed atomistically. The classical empiricist sought this through the (mistaken) view that ordinary, daily experience actually was atomized. But by telling us mistakenly that it already was such, they taught us to re-interpret in an atomized manner. This ratifies and confirms the scientific habit of not taking old clusters of ideas for granted and, instead, experimentally rearranging and disaggregating them.

This 'experience only' clause gives the empiricist theory a very powerful cutting edge. The denial of other sources of knowledge implies distrust of any background ideas and pictures which dominate or influence the interpretation of observation. It firmly precludes their entrenchment in the reserved, fundamental beliefs of the culture. *It places cultures on trial.*

There is perhaps no way of excluding the use of background pictures altogether; but once it is recognized that none of them are sacrosanct, there is then no justification for granting them permanent, indefinite authority over the data which seem to go against them. It may be fair enough to ignore or explain away a few facts which could cause despair in Billancourt, or even in some scholarly community; but enough is enough. There comes a point, which it may not be possible to define formally, when despair in Billancourt, or anywhere else, ceases to be a legitimate counter-argument. In the end, the data base trumps any psychic or social need, and any general picture linked to it.

What was crucial in empiricist theory was the implicit systematization and equalization of all concepts: none was sacrosanct. All of them were expected to conform to the same code of conduct, and submit to the same trial. Men had always been sensitive to experience and nature, and it is probable that primitive man in certain ways had rather more of such sensitivity than members of more sophisticated cultures, whose scholars often possess somewhat atrophied physical sensibilities. If sensitivity to nature were all that was required for culture-transcending knowledge, the attainment of science would have been granted to mankind long ago.

But it was *not* enough. What was needed was that the fruits of this sensitivity be recorded in an idiom which was tidy and symmetrical, and which systematically cross-connects all information, tests generalizations at all possible points, which links the data to general questions and does so with precision, and which relates various issues to each other in a shared, standardized, and precise currency. It also required a strong drive to even greater systematization and unification. In other words, concepts and cognitive claims had to behave in that sober, symmetrical, even-headed, systematic way that Max Weber credited to the comportment and the sensibility of the adherents of puritanism, and which thereby allegedly gave birth to rational and cumulative production.

So it was this aspect of rationalism, in the sense of a stress on methodicalness and order and symmetry, the pursuit of rules-without-exceptions, which turned a mere empirical sensibility from one low-powered thing-amongst-others, into the powerful instrument which it now is. There clearly is a parallel between this and what Weber taught us about greed. There had always been greed amongst men, and no doubt some men had often been possessed by greed to the exclusion of other concerns. But it was not greed which engendered capitalism and rational production: it was the *disciplining* of greed, its ruthless taming by order and calculation, and its conversion into a curiously disinterested compulsion, indulged for its own sake rather than for its fruits, which really did the trick. A Marxist such as Marshall Sahlins holds that men were not always greedy, but that it was greed which engendered an avaricious world, from which presumably we may one day escape again.[1] By contrast, Weber can allow that greed was ever present, whether or not dominant, but is obliged to insist that on its own, it remained quite incapable of engendering our systematically acquisitive world. Only disciplined, disinterested, *ascetic* greed could do that.

Something similar holds of sensitivity. The empiricists vaunt experience. What really mattered was not what they assert about experience as such, but what they tacitly took for granted, and quietly presupposed, in their account of how experience should be handled. They were already puritans and, in a rather literal sense, methodists. They took for granted the orderly systematization of sensitivity. It was at this point, in their tacit assumption of symmetry and order in our procedures, and not in the invocation of experience as such, that the real secret of high-powered modern knowledge is to be found. It was their rationalist, methodical, orderly, puritan tacit assumptions, not their

---

[1] M. Sahlins, *Stone Age Economics* (Tavistock, London, 1974).

sensualist empiricist slogans, which gave their doctrines their real power, their cutting edge.

Rationalism in effect contained an answer to the much-vaunted 'theory-saturation of fact' problem, which is supposed to invalidate the empiricist model of knowledge. The rationalist prescriptions of *atomization* of issues, of replication and symmetry, jointly prevent the perpetual self-preservation of theories by perpetually injecting them into perceived facts. If the associations or interpretations which accompany perception are themselves repeatedly scrutinized from diverse viewpoints, by breaking up their support into their experimental atoms, then self-maintaining circles of ideas do not survive, and knowledge can grow.

There is a striking, and of course far from accidental, parallel between all this and the ethical theory most closely associated with empiricism, namely utilitarianism. This widely influential theory shares the logic and the spirit of empiricism. It claimed that the only legitimate arbiter of our values was human contentment, happiness, pleasure. A philosophy for pigs! – growled its critics. Not at all: it was a philosophy for puritans. The real centre of gravity of this theory lay not in its near-tautological stress on happiness, which was an almost vacuous label attached to any preferred experience; but rather, in its rationalist reluctance to accept inherited views, and an insistence that human values must instead be based on freshly re-examined, genuine human preferences. It was located in the insistence that human needs be examined in an egalitarian, symmetrical, methodical manner, with each man counting for one and no more than one. Human needs and desires were to be examined in that same cool, analytic, step-by-step spirit, with which the empiricist investigator dismembered traditional visions of *nature*. It was the subjection of cultural custom to a philosophical Auditor, professionally obliged to scrutinize whether current social arrangements really extracted most pleasure and least pain from available resources, which turned utilitarianism into a socially radical, indeed revolutionary, agency. Underneath the language of what seems to be the brazen sensualist, there was the spirit of the Methodist... Scratch an empiricist, find a rationalist.

Reason against Passion

The early rationalists endeavoured to deploy reason not merely in the accumulation of truths, but also in the conduct of life. Their idea of the cognitive good life was one of open-ended accumulation, but in the sphere of morals their ideal was rather one of rational adaptation, of stoical acceptance. The moral philosophy found in early rationalists such as Descartes and Spinoza is one of trimming the sails of our desires to the prevailing winds, of finding contentment in adjustment to reality, rather than striving to bend reality to our will. The supposition that the world would be transformed so that *it* should please *us*, so conspicuous in the world which rationalism eventually engendered, was then largely absent. That only came when the enhancement of technological power encouraged men to bend nature to our desires, by showing it to be surprisingly easy.

The later empiricist crypto-rationalists, who were technically, superficially sensualists, in reality saw morality much as an accountant would see it. The maximal output of units of satisfaction was to be attained and then sensibly distributed, in accordance with some rational, acceptable and egalitarian principle. But above all, the total sum was to be expanded, radically expanded, and no limit was set to this expansion. It was expected to be very substantial, and so in the event it proved to be. In brief, the collective pursuit of sensual satisfaction was anything rather than wild and orgiastic; it was sober, systematic, and orderly. In the country of its birth, sensualist utilitarianism led not to an orgy, but to the welfare state, and to its agent the social worker.

The question arises: can such a pursuit of satisfaction-maximization, or alternatively the implementation of principle for principle's sake, ever genuinely satisfy the human spirit? John Stuart Mill in his celebrated and autobiographically recorded depression found that it could not.[1] Happiness could not be striven for directly; it could only be the by-product of the attainment of other ends. But we cannot simply trick ourselves into happiness by setting ourselves other ends, and then shiftily savouring contentment when they are attained – without ever admitting to ourselves that it was the contentment as such, and not the specific aims, we wanted. We cannot choose our aims. They choose us. Man can do as he will, but he cannot will as he will – as Schopenhauer observed.

What kind of aims *really* have a hold over us? They seem to be linked to our powerful quasi-biological drives of sex, domination, power, membership of an effective community, resentment. Though linked to these urges, our desires assume their specific form in terms of long-term, intimate, and unconscious personal relations. Human life is played out within these intimate, hidden, and highly personal constellations; our satisfaction and dissatisfaction is determined by these obscure reactions, which would appall, dismay, and bewilder any orderly accountant. They defy orderly calculation. They are professionally handled, if at all, by the shaman-like, secretive, and evasive depth therapist, rather than the hedonic accountant. We know not what we do, we know not why we do it, we know not what makes us content and what drives us to despair, and we have little real understanding of the situations in which we find ourselves, of the genuine emotive charge which our environment holds for us.

This, at any rate, is the important germ of truth in the fashionable depth psychology of the twentieth century, however nebulous, flabby and evasive its more specific and theoretical doctrines, and however baseless its therapeutic claims. Our conscious mind seems to be rather like the public relations department of a large, complex and turbulent firm, dominated by a secretive and divided management, which never allows the PR officer to be privy to its secrets. Public Relations content themselves with issuing idealized and simplified accounts of the

[1] J.S. Mill, *Autobiography* (London, 1873).

situation for external consumption, and these bear little relation to the real state of affairs within the corporation, and have little influence on it. Cartesian, Humeian, and Kantian philosophy more or less correctly codified the cognitive ethic of a new civilization. But as an account of the intimate psychic life of its individual members, it is worthless.

Freud is widely and plausibly credited with the discovery that man is not master in his own house. This idea is perfectly valid, even if the part of Freud's teaching which claims to provide even a modest increase in that mastery is spurious. The self-image of modern rational man, citizen of the unique society engendered by the great outburst of cognitive and productive rationality, is indebted more to the ideas and terminology of Freud than it is to any other single source. Rational man had rediscovered his own irrationality, characterized it in a naturalist idiom, and is told he can communicate with and appease his own irrational roots by a procedure which respects his individualism (the ritual is in most cases not collective but solitary), and achieve insight not by orderly, clear, and distinct ideas, but through a kind of conceptual abandon, through 'pre-association', which inverts all his habitual intellectual practices and obligations. Psychoanalysis requires, and revels in, an orgy of conceptual antinomianism. It claims to be the only route of access to the Deep and hence to salvation.

In modern irrationalism, a number of plausible themes are liable to blend. There is the depth-psychological view of the murky, devious, and instinctual nature of our real satisfaction, far removed from our alleged fulfilment either in abstract ideals, or even in rational greed. There is also the perception that our life is lived, not in the single-minded pursuit of clearly formulated aims, but as the playing out of an endorsed and recognized role in a culture and community, and that such membership and acceptance is not subject to cost-benefit calculation. When economic growth tapers off (not because no further inventions are possible, but because there is no real further pay-off), there may be much less room for instrumental rationality. It is not merely that growth needs rationality, but rationality needs growth. It can best be deployed in the unstable pursuit of new opportunities. When growth ceases, or ceases to be important, rationality may also lose its significance. In the re-stabilized social order which may come when technology no longer enhances our options, multi-stranded arrangements may curtail the zone in which 'reason' can be freely deployed. In a stable or re-stabilized culture, the ruthless pursuit of a single end would be liable to disturb too many many-sided adjustments. Only in periods of growth can a severe separation of the productive sphere really be tolerated. If society becomes re-established, rationality may return to its erstwhile ghetto, and custom recover its empire.

There is also the consideration that rational assessment is possible for given options, if much of the background is taken as fixed; but major political decisions in modern society are taken against a background which is itself in flux and *sub judice*. The number of incommensurate considerations which enter major decisions is too large and disparate to allow their reduction to some single measure. Major issues no longer appear on the political or even economic agenda twice because, in a complex and rapidly changing technical and social environment, no situation is really repeated; hence there is no clear sense in which one can learn from experience. All these considerations, jointly and severally, help weaken the rationalist ideal in spheres other than cognition. So, in stability or flux, reason is now in peril.

9
Recapitulation

The human species has, by some evolutionary mechanism not yet properly understood, developed an astonishing volatility of response. This absence of genetic pre-programming has engendered the need to be constrained socially and conceptually, as a compensation of our volatility: if reaction-systems were really accumulated at random by individual association, and by reaction to idiosyncratic experience, as empiricism had taught, neither a semantic nor a social order would be possible. Meanings and reactions would be too chaotic and unpredictable. No such polymorphous, unstable species could possibly have survived. Providentially, the capacity to respond to social-semantic restraints on conduct has emerged at the same time as the behavioural plasticity. Had it not, we should not be here.

This was part of Durkheim's insight. Socially imposed, internalized compulsion was essential, if we were to be capable of thought, communication, cohesion, and cooperation. Rationality, in the first, Durkheimian or generic sense, can be equated with the submission to socially shared, communally distinctive, and compulsively internalized concepts. In the beginning there was the prohibition. Language is an astonishingly rich system of socially instilled markers, capable of helping to keep members of a community within their cultural bounds or at least indicating what the bounds are; but the built-in genuine principles of language are such that countless languages and cultures are possible. This in turn makes possible cultural diversity, and hence a rate of change far more rapid than genetic transformation on its own could ever be.

The socially instilled concepts generally serve multiple purposes and, like the men who carry them, fail to observe any very orderly and developed division of labour. They are so to speak poly-functional. They are only rational in the Durkheimian sense: they are socially instilled, and make both cohesion and comprehension possible, by endowing members of a semantic community with the *same* compulsions. They impose both logical and moral order on men.

But they are irrational in the narrower or Weberian sense of rationality: they are not methodical, and they do not serve single, insulated and clearly articulated ends, which alone can permit an accurate assessment of instrumental efficiency. They are not all subject to the same laws; they often serve multiple ends, are subject to plural constraints, and so cannot serve any one of them with ruthless single-mindedness and calculable effect. Though sensitivity to extraneous natural fact is often present, it is almost always but one element amongst many; it is not tidily insulated, nor dominant. In other words, language is not primarily referential, and those parts of it which are referential are not exclusively so. There is no single idiom, no single conceptual currency, which would enable the entire wealth of assertion to be cross-connected and systematized and expanded.

As long as the conceptual life of mankind had this so to speak Durkheimian form, there could be no question of limitless and effective exploration of nature. Similarly, there could be no question of that sustained innovation in productive techniques, in the combination of elements of production, which leads to sustained economic growth. Needless to say, there could also be no question of the combination of these two forms of expansion of human life, and the emergence of a society based on growth and progress. On the contrary, the intellectual life of human societies was an integral part of a tendency to self-perpetuation. In general, it underwrote the stagnation-sustaining domination of agrarian humanity by an alliance of specialists in coercion and in ritual.

The transition from the first, generic rationality of Durkheim, to the more specific rationality which obsessed Weber, is perhaps the biggest single event in human history. We do not really know how it came about, and perhaps we never shall. We do, however, possess, in the work of Max Weber, one fascinating and suggestive hypothesis. Even if in the end it proves false, it has the inestimable merit of highlighting the problem forcefully. The answer, whether or not correct, endows the question with a sharp outline. It helps us understand the distinctiveness of our situation.

The world so engendered contained both rational production and cognition. The rules of both were in due course codified. Two Scotsmen, Hume and Smith, put it all down, one of them taking on cognition, and the other, production. Their views on coercion converged, and they were indeed friends.

In this way the notion of a single, systematic, orderly method of the attainment of truth, incarnate in all and privileged in none, was rounded off, and accorded the name of Reason. It was of course in conflict with the residual element of the privileged-sacred view of things, perpetuated by the very theology which had also brought about the new vision in the first place. This conflict, more than any other, made familiar the notion of Reason. The notion of the exclusive, jealous and orderly deity, which had helped engender rational unificatory thought, itself in the end also sinned against it. The privileged claim that the deity existed, not to mention various more specific and sometimes weird affirmations which remained attached to it, could in the end no longer satisfy the criteria of reason. Reason destroyed its own progenitor. Parricide can now be added to the list of its crimes. It is parricidal as well as impotent and suicidal.

Modern irrationalists are much addicted to the *tu quoque* argument: Reason cannot justify her own procedures without circularity: so are we not all equal, all equally guilty of the sin of circularity and prejudgement? But the rationalist may rightly object to being placed at the same level as the believers. He may well say to them, as the Catholic Church used to say to the Protestants in pre-ecumenical days – you are many, we are one. The carte blanche provided by generic irrationalism validates *all* faiths, the path prescribed by Reason is unique. The *tu quoque* argument justifies all faiths equally, and not any single one of them. It blesses all of them alike, including all possible and as yet unborn beliefs. In as far as it is an argument at all, it leads, not to genuine conviction, but to an unbridled doctrinal permissiveness.

The *tu quoque* argument brings us to the next stage in the story of Reason. After parricide comes impotence. Descartes and the early rationalists had hoped to deliver their new tool, Reason, as a product Guaranteed by the Makers, not for a year, but for all eternity. The Warranty was to be valid forever. Descartes had indeed been impelled to his efforts to guarantee this tool precisely because other producers of truths were supplying such unutterably shabby goods, accompanied by notoriously boastful, vainglorious, menacingly vindictive, and blatantly mendacious and untrustworthy warranties. Ancient sages sought watertight life-styles, safe from disappointment. Descartes was also determined to market only goods of the highest quality, accompanied by a totally honest and trustworthy guarantee, though, unlike the sages of old, he sought a foolproof method of inquiry rather than a foolproof life-style. Spinoza adapted his new ideas to the old quest for a self-guaranteeing life-style.

First came the discovery that Reason could not really provide any such warranty. The Impotence of Reason is itself an independent truth of reason. Hume showed that the clear and distinct data did not permit a cogent inference to the kind of world we in fact inhabit and manipulate. A system of inquiry which is effective in the exploration of nature, by breaking up questions and the atomization of evidence and the pursuit of order, cannot, from within its own resources, or without contravening its own principles, establish that such an inquiry *must* be successful. And after impotence came suicide. Reason engenders a unitary, naturalistic world, within which there is no real place for Reason.

Modern irrationalism is by now very seldom the expression of a genuine devotion to extra-rational, extra-natural Authority. That particular debate, between protagonists of Authority and partisans of Free Thought, though not wholly dead, is largely antiquated. In as far as it continues at all, it is muted, and much overlaid by other considerations. The important enemies of reason no longer loudly claim to have access to a source of revelation outside the world. They claim that, *within* the natural world, as laid bare by reason, there are authorities more legitimate than reason, so that reason should not, or cannot, be heeded. Cognition, valuation, social organization, are and ought really to be slaves of intra-mundane forces, whom reason serves not merely as slave, but also as façade or camouflage. Freud's charge of the practice of sustained disinformation was added to Hume's attribution of inherent slavery. The new attack on reason commends not transcendent, but only this-worldly rival authorities. Tradition, earth, blood, the Dialectic, are the new rivals: they speak from within the world, and not outside it.

One might also divide the problems of human reason into the predicament of insanity and the predicament of divinity. Reason can be abandoned, on the one hand, because the forces which in fact control us are so complex, powerful and mysterious that we cannot aspire either to understand or to master them. A puny vessel with a feeble instrument of propulsion, launched into a powerful and turbulent current, has no prospects – other than, perhaps, going with the current and hoping for the best. It would be idle to pretend that such an account of our condition, individually or collectively, is far removed from the truth. This is the problem of insanity: a man seized by inner forces too strong and too incomprehensible to master, cannot control his own fate. Descartes's rules cannot help a man fight psychotic delusions: and it is *only* luck, not some rational merit, which saves any of us from such a condition.

But, ironically, some of the problems of reason spring from the opposite consideration. It is unclear what reasons the Deity could conceivably have had for creating the world as it is: neither aims nor facts nor laws were imposed on It, and consequently it could not have had any conceivable reason for creating *this* rather than *that*. Lacking constraints, It also lacked any possible reason for doing one thing rather than another. The deity is deprived of the succour of the Principle of Sufficient Reason. The intellectual condition of advanced humanity has in some measure come to resemble this condition. In as far as social, genetic, and other engineering turns human traits, including values, into manipulable variables rather than, as once they were, fixed data, we find in ourselves similarly premiss-less conditions. Reason simply is not capable of providing the premisses which could select or establish either our aims or our means. Impotence of reasoning may be the obverse of technological power. In a world dominated by an effective science and technology, and a highly variable and manipulable society and humanity, we simply lack sufficient premisses for long-term policy decisions. Too much knowledge erodes our premisses, or should we say – it erodes the old illusion of fixed premisses. Our past constraints had limited our options, and our superstitions endowed our constrained options with the illusion of legitimacy. Our new powers leave us free-floating. We may find ourselves in a kind of premiss-less vacuum, with too much power to create, and no reasons for choice concerning what we create. Practical men of action, notoriously living from hand to mouth under constant pressure, may find this an improbable danger. It is a real one none the less. Technological near-omnipotence has its own perils. Strangely enough, they complement those of subjection to incomprehensible forces. The fear of insanity and of divinity can be relevant to the same situation.

The claims of unreason are not equally persuasive in all spheres. They are not very persuasive in cognition, notwithstanding the fact that the absence of a warranty for rational procedures is undeniable. Cognition continues to function admirably, even given the absence of any such guarantee. In production, the claims of unreason, still far from persuasive, are somewhat stronger. In our human self-image and self-assessment, the claims of unreason appear to be overwhelmingly strong, though it is not very clear just how we should live by the contrary, irrationalist vision. Its oracles speak in nebulous and murky language, and their pronouncements are allergic to clarity. In practice, we make do with makeshift compromises.

The early rationalists had supposed Reason to be endowed not merely with an absolute and eternal warranty, but also to be a most powerful universal tool, usable in all spheres. It turns out not merely that the warranty is lacking, but also that the tool, though effective in some spheres, is ineffectual or counter-productive in others. It is of no great help in the business of living, individually or collectively.

After the language of cultural transcendence, there came the Providentialism of Hegel and his progeny, including Marx, and many others. That was simply a fantasy. World history is not a story designed for our benefit, edification, and fulfilment; nor is the world which has emerged with rationality a necessary culmination, or the best of all possible worlds. It has some great merits, and some major defects, and we need to explore both. It only emerged by chance, and there is a heavy price to be paid for the material and social perks it unquestionably offers. The siege mentality introduced by Max Weber – it all emerged by a precarious accident, and the cost is great – is incomparably superior to the complacency of the Hegelo-Marxist tradition. We need to understand both our precariousness and our options, and their price. We can do without the illusion that we are the legitimate heirs, the final end, culmination and purpose of global development, and that it had been designed specifically to produce us. This form of philosophic megalomania we can leave to the Hegelians and their intellectual offspring.

In a stable traditional world, men had identities, linked to their social roles, and confirmed by their overall vision of nature and society. Instability and rapid change both in knowledge and in society has deprived such self-images of their erstwhile feel of reliability. Identities are perhaps more ironic and conditional than once they were, or at any rate, when confident, unjustifiably so. But the very style of knowing which has effected this erosion of confidence is also the basis of a new and different kind of identity. We could in the end seek our identity in Reason, and find it in a style of thought which gives us what genuine knowledge of the world we have, and which enjoins us to treat each other equitably – notwithstanding the lady's mundane roots, precarious base, unequal performance, failure to legitimate herself, and her marked parricidal and suicidal tendencies.

Select Bibliography

1 Texts

Bartley, W.W. III, *The Retreat to Commitment*, 2nd edn, La Salle, London, 1984.
Benda, J., *La Trahison des clercs*, Grasset, Paris, 1927.
Berlin, I., *Four Essays on Liberty*, Oxford University Press, Oxford, 1968.
Chomsky, N., *Cartesian Linguistics*, Harper and Row, New York and London, 1966.
——, *Knowledge of Language: Its nature, origin and use*, Praeger, New York, 1986.
——, *Language and Responsibility*, Harvester, Brighton, 1979.
——, *Reflections on Language*, Temple Smith, London, 1976.
Collingwood, R.G., *An Autobiography*, Oxford University Press, Oxford, 1939; repr. 1970.
Descartes, R., *Discourse on Method* (1637), in *The Philosophical Writings of Descartes*, tr. J. Cottingham, R. Stoothoff and D. Murdoch, 2 vols, Cambridge University Press, Cambridge, 1985.
——, *The Principles of Philosophy* (1644), in *The Philosophical Writings of Descartes*, tr. J. Cottingham, R. Stoothoff and D. Murdoch, 2 vols, Cambridge University Press, Cambridge, 1985.
Durkheim, E., *The Elementary Forms of the Religious Life: A study in religious sociology* (1912), tr. Joseph Ward Swain, Allen and Unwin, London, 1915, repr. 1976.
Feyerabend, P., *Against Method*, NLB, London, 1975.
Frazer, J.G., *The Golden Bough: A study in magic and religion*, 16 vols, 3rd edn, Macmillan, London, 1913, repr, 1990.
Hegel, G.W.F., *Lectures on the Philosophy of World History* (1837), Cambridge University Press, Cambridge, 1975.
Hume, D., *A Treatise of Human Nature* (1739), ed. L.A. Selby-Bigge, 2nd edn 1978, Clarendon Press, Oxford.

James, W., *Pragmatism: A new name for some old ways of thinking*, Longmans, New York, 1907.

Kant, I., *The Critique of Pure Reason* (1781), in *Immanuel Kant's Critique of Pure Reason*, tr. N. Kemp Smith, Macmillan, London, 1953.

Marx, K., *Theses on Feuerbach*, in K. Marx and F. Engels, *The German Ideology*, Lawrence and Wishart, London, 1938, 1942; repr. 1965.

—— and F. Engels, *The German Ideology*, parts I and II, Lawrence and Wishart, London, 1938, 1942; repr. 1965.

Mill, J.S., *Autobiography* (1873).

Newman, J., *Apologia pro Vita Sua* (1865), ed. M.J. Svaglic, Clarendon Press, London, 1967.

Pascal, B., *Pensées* (1670), J. Delmas, Paris, 1960.

Popper, K.R., *The Logic of Scientific Discovery*, Hutchinson, London, 1959.

Quine, W.V.O., *From a Logical Point of View*, Harvard University Press, Cambridge, MA, 1953.

——, *Ontological Relativity and Other Essays*, Columbia University Press, New York and London, 1969.

Schopenhauer, A., *The World as Will and Representation* (1818), 2 vols, tr. E.F.J. Payne, Dover, New York, 1966.

Spinoza, B., *De Intellectus Emendatione* (1677), in *Ethics and De Intellectus Emendatione*, Dent, London, 1910.

Stendhal, *De l'amour*, Le Divan, Paris, 1927.

Weber, M., *The Protestant Ethic and the Spirit of Capitalism*, tr. Talcott Parsons, Unwin University Books, London, 1930, repr. 1965.

Wittgenstein, L., *Philosophical Investigations*, tr. G.E.M. Anscombe, Blackwell, Oxford, 1968.

——, *Tractatus Logico-Philosophicus*, tr. C.K. Ogden (1922; repr. 1923 with corrections).

2   Secondary works

Barth, K., *A Shorter Commentary on Romans*, SCM Press, London, 1959.

Bell, D., *The Cultural Contradictions of Capitalism*, Heinemann, London, 1976.

Brubaker, R., *The Limits of Rationality: An essay on the social and moral thought of Max Weber*, Allen and Unwin, London, 1984.

d'Agostino, F., *Chomsky's System of Ideas*, Clarendon Press, Oxford, 1986.

Dore, R., *British Factory, Japanese Factory*, Allen and Unwin, London, 1973.

Gellner, E., *The Psychoanalytic Movement: Or the cunning of unreason*, Paladin, London, 1985.

Giddens, A., *Durkheim*, Fontana, London, 1978.

Kuhn, T., *The Structure of Scientific Revolutions*, 2nd imp, University of Chicago Press, Chicago, 1963.

Lakatos, I., 'Falsification and the methodology of scientific research programmes', in *Criticism and the Growth of Knowledge*, ed. I. Lakatos and A. Musgrave, Cambridge University Press, Cambridge, 1970.

Lecky, W.E.H., *History of the Rise and Influence of the Spirit of Rationalism in Europe*, Longmans, Green, London, 1910.

Luhrmann, T., *Persuasions of the Witch's Craft: Ritual magic and witchcraft in present-day England*, Blackwell, Oxford, 1989.

Lukes, S., *Emile Durkheim: His life and work*, Harper and Row, New York and London, 1973.

Magee, B., *The Great Philosophers: An introduction to Western philosophy*, BBC Books, London, 1987.

——, *Men of Ideas: Some creators of contemporary philosophy*, BBC Books, London, 1978.

——, *The Philosophy of Schopenhauer*, Clarendon Press, Oxford, 1983.

—— (ed.), *Modern British Philosophy*, Oxford University Press, Oxford, 1971, repr. 1986.

Marcuse, H., *Reason and Revolution: Hegel and the rise of social theory*, Oxford University Press, Oxford, 1941; repr. Routledge and Kegan Paul, London, 1955.

Mossner, E.C., *The Life of David Hume*, 2nd edn, Clarendon Press, Oxford, 1980.

Oakeshott, M., *On Human Conduct*, Clarendon Press, Oxford, 1975.

——, *Rationalism in Politics and Other Essays*, Methuen, London, 1962.

Popkin, R., 'The third force in seventeenth-century thought: scepticism, science and millenarianism', in *The Prism of Science*, ed. E. Ullman-Margalit, Boston Studies in the Philosophy of Science, vol. 95, D. Reidel, Boston, 1986.

Sahlins, M., *Stone Age Economics*, Tavistock, London, 1974.

Schluchter, W., *The Rise of Western Rationalism: Max Weber's developmental history*, tr. Guenther Roth, University of California Press, Berkeley and London, 1981.

Tiryakian, E.E., 'A problem in the sociology of knowledge: the mutual unawareness of Emile Durkheim and Max Weber', *European Journal of Sociology*, 7.2, 1960.

Wrigley, E.A., *People, Cities and Wealth: The transformation of traditional society*, Blackwell, Oxford, 1987.

Index

Absolute Spirit, in Hegel, 78–9, 81–2
absolutism, scientific, 114, 165
abstractions, role in history, 80
accumulation, in capitalism, 139, 170; cultural, 77, 155, 172
aestheticism, 85, 88
America, United States, and Pragmatism, 99–100
animals, mental life, 37
anthropology, and conceptual compulsion, 31–6
art, and rationality, 150
association, 31, 33–6, 37, 125–6; free, 33, 94–6
atomization, 167, 168, 171, 179
autarchy, intellectual, 3, 157–9, 163
authoritarianism, in science, 114
authority, and Reason, 52, 58–62, 63, 70, 90, 92, 98, 102–3, 137, 179–80
autonomy, and Reason, 5–6, 155–63, 164

behaviourism, 64–5
belief, and association, 35; and

rationality, 60–2, 63, 146, 151–2
Bell, D., 146n.
Benda, Julien, 129–32
Berlin, Sir Isaiah, 135
biology, and naturalization of man, 97–8, 100; role in philosophy, 86–7
Bloch, Marc, ix–x

capitalism, and production, 139–43, 155–6; and Protestantism 6, 46–8, 170
causality, in Durkheim, 31; in Hume, xii, 21, 53; in Kant, 32–3
change, social, 135, 177, 182
charisma, 152–3
Chomsky, Noam, 64, 124–8, 134
Christianity, and authority, 58
civilization, and Reason, 136, 138
classicism, of Descartes, 4, 6, 13
coercion, 80–1, 152–3, 160, 177–8
cognition, and autonomy, 155–63, 164; and culture, 18–19, 24; in Descartes; 9–12,

growth, cognitive, 19; as
corruption, 4–5, 57
guild, in Freud, 89, 90, 96

Harmony, Pre-established,
98–102, 160
Hegel, G.W.F., and Culture, 77,
182; and historical
materialism, 79–82, 87, 98; on
latent function, 76–8; on
progress, 75–6; on the rational
and the natural, 73, 74, 76,
78–9, 84
history, and growth of
rationality, 74, 81–2, 98; and
latent function, 76–8; and
materialism, 79–81, 87; and
Progress, 75–6, 99–100; and
Revelation 24, 78
Hume, David, and cognition,
13–16, 20–2, 24–7, 29, 32, 35,
37, 178; critique, 30, 31; on
experience, 67–9; on morality,
135; and Reason, xii, 53, 63–4,
71, 131, 133, 179–80; on the
self, 22–3, 70; on truth, 57

idea, in Descartes, 4–5, 9–12,
13–14, 17, 25, 147;
falsification, 107–9; in Hume,
14–15, 20–1, 27; and ritual,
42; see also association
identity, in Existentialism, 130;
in Freud, 89–90; and Nature,
83–182; and self, 69–70, 74;
and work, 140
impression, in Hume, 13, 15, 20,
24, 27
individualism, and irrationality,
174; and rationalism, 3–4,
5–6, 8, 13–16, 18, 72, 73,

160–2; and rise of capitalism,
44; and science, 112
inductivism, 112
inference, vindication, 105–11
insanity, 180–1
intellectuals, and commitment,
129–32
interpretation, and perception,
167
intuition, and Reason, 66–7
irrationalism, 82, 90–3, 132–5,
180–2; and culture, 150; and
intellectuals, 131–2; in Kuhn,
112–15; and language, 126–8,
177; political, 153–4; and
Reason and Nature, 97–8,
102–5; and science, 109–10,
147; therapeutic, 93–6, 174;
and *tu quoque* argument, 147,
165, 178–9; in Wittgenstein,
116–23

James, William, 100

Kant, Immanuel, on cognition,
22–3, 24–8, 32–3, 36–7; in
Durkheim, 30; on morality
and experience, 68–9, 74; on
Nature and Reason, 82–3; and
Reason, xii, 13, 29, 73–4, 154;
on the self, 22–3, 26, 68, 70,
73–4, 84, 87
Kuhn, Thomas, 112–15, 133

Lakatos, I., 110
language, in Chomsky, 64,
124–8, 134; games, 133–4; and
social control, 149, 176–7; in
Wittgenstein, 117–23, 124,
133–4

Index compiled by Meg Davies (Society of Indexers)